—ENGLISH COTTAGES—
TONY EVANS AND CANDIDA LYCETT GREEN

INTRODUCTION BY
JOHN BETJEMAN

A STUDIO BOOK · THE VIKING PRESS · NEW YORK

Half title page: Wilby, Stradbroke, Suffolk
Title page: Horton Cross, Ilminster, Somerset

Photographs copyright © Tony Evans 1982
Text and captions copyright © Candida Lycett Green 1982
Introduction copyright © John Betjeman 1982

Second Printing June 1983

Published in 1983 by The Viking Press (A Studio Book)
625 Madison Avenue, New York, N.Y. 10022

Published simultaneously in Canada
by Penguin Books Canada Limited

Library of Congress Catalog Card Number: 82–050271

ISBN: 0–670–29670–8

Designer: John Gorham
Editorial Director: Mark Boxer

Printed and bound in Italy by L.E.G.O. Vicenza

CONTENTS

HARPFORD,
NEWTON POPPLEFORD,
DEVONSHIRE

This book is by no means comprehensive, but is an attempt to show the cottage heritage of England as being the most varied and beautiful in the world. In general the cottages included befit their dictionary definition of 'a small and humble dwelling', but we have also included what were referred to as cottages in the 18th and 19th centuries, though small and humble they certainly weren't. We have ignored new county boundaries and the new nomenclature such as Humberside for part of Yorkshire. Cottages and villages are captioned throughout the book as being in the counties to which they have always belonged, rather than the new counties in which they are officially placed. The nearest town has been included should any muddle arise. CLG

I would like to thank the following people for their suggestions, help and advice: James Ayres, William Bulwer-Long, Roy Carter, Claire Charlton, John Cornforth, Rachel Crutch, Gillian Darley, The Duchess of Devonshire, Anna Eadon, The Rev. John Ford, Christopher Gibbs, Mark Girouard, John and Jane Goman, Eileen Harris, Lady Harrod, David Hicks, Rodney Hollick, Gervaise Jackson-Stops, Diana Keast, Lady Lasdun, Lucy Lycett Green, Zara Maxwell-Hyslop, David Mlinaric, Christopher Morris, John Nankivell, The National Trust, Guy Nevill, Andrew Parker Bowles, John Pentney, Denys Scott, Alistair Service, Gavin Stamp, Frederick Stockdale, Sir Tatton Sykes, Lady Emma Tennant, Nigel Thimbleby, The Rev. Henry Thorold, Lady Juliet Townsend, David Vicary, Queenie Weaver, Jock Williamson, Kate Woodason, and The Hon. Mark Wyndham. CLG

I am most grateful to the following people for their help and kindness to me while I was taking the photographs: Jill Abraham, Bessie Abrey, Diane Aubrey, Frank and Grace Blackmore, Mr and Mrs Noel Carrington, Margaret Charlton, Susan Denyer, John and Voline Dickson, Lionel and Marion Diplock, Ronnie and Rose Marie Duncan, John and Joan Firth, Mr and Mrs Donald Gimson, Alan and Lorna Harding, Mr and Mrs Richard Hargreaves, Alex and Gloria Harrison, Henry at the kennels, Guy and Nick Hodgkinson, Mr and Mrs Ed Huckett, Robert and Kirstie Law, Doug and Sue Maxwell, Beryl Murdoch, the Nixons of Ambleside, Patricia and Damion Parsons, Brian Rice, Patrick and Sandra Stagg, Greta Thomson, the Weeks brothers, Leslie Weeks, Kathleen Witt, Joanne and Peter Wright, Robin Wright, and not forgetting the driver who let me highjack his lorry and the lady who ran up the Union Jack in Sidmouth. TE

Eland is a constant delight because of its rapid change of scene; almost within a few hundred yards the character of a place changes. That is why building materials tell us where we are.

Looking at buildings can still be a pleasure provided we disregard the classifying of them into categories and dates, but just look at them for themselves and their setting. Whether it is a half-timbered cottage built in the 13th century at Alfriston in Sussex or a half-timbered cottage built in 1906 at Godalming in Surrey does not really matter.

Although this book covers only England, far more achitectural influence in the 18th and 19th centuries than most people imagine came from Scotland – from men like the Adam brothers, Lorimer and Mackintosh, and from Wales – from men such as John Nash, whose practice began at Carmarthen and continued into the 20th century, and later, the innovating architects North and Padmore. There is no doubt that their influence reached cottage architecture. Neither must the Isle of Man be forgotten, where, from the Georgian front of Douglas to the Arts and Crafts cottages by Baillie Scott, there is no lack of variety. (Baillie Scott in fact was so sea-sick on his journey over to the Island that he remained there for a long time summoning up the courage to go back. He is said to have held an exhibition of his drawings there and some of the pictures he hung upside down because he thought they looked nicer that way.)

My daughter is quite right when she says that people think their cottages are far older than they are, but the first cottages were no more than shelters for human bodies against the elements, and architecture did not come in until the 18th century and then not consciously. I have seen the sole black house in these islands on the island of Foula beyond the outer Hebrides; it had no windows and the place was full of smoke from a fire lighted in the middle of the room. This was what early cottages were like before people improved themselves. From solidified tents to the village street and on to the pre-fab, the process is continuous. The great houses remain aloof and alone, but this book contains the ordinary houses – the cottages that we all dream of having.

In stone districts human beings and cattle were housed under one roof, and two storeys were a rarity. Many a past village has been discovered through aerial photography showing up field patterns. In 1349 the Black Death wiped out a third of England's

BERRYNARBOR, ILFRACOMBE, DEVONSHIRE

Isolated cottages such as this one tucked tidily into the Devon landscape would have been farms in their earlier days. There are more than twenty thousand farm sites in Devon and perhaps that is why there are more roads and lanes in the county than in the whole of Belgium. All cottages were originally thatched; but because of extensive fires, particularly at Tavistock, which was burned to the ground three times, cautious Devonians began to re-roof their homes with slate.

WELCOMBE, HARTLAND, DEVONSHIRE

Sheltered from the storms that beat so close along a treacherous stretch of North Devonshire coast, this whitewashed stone cottage was a working mill in the last century. In his *Highways and Byways in Devon and Cornwall* (1897), Arthur Norway describes coming upon it while walking from Morwenstow to Hartland: '. . . the brown stream which sings out of golden woods higher up the valley, turns a mill on the open ground near the sea; and here also is a sawpit in which two men are working busily. The sharp scent of the sawdust is blown up where I stand among the furze . . . The men stop working, the children run out of the mill to see the stranger. It is their one excitement. In this season it may be three weeks ere another comes.' The cottage now belongs to the poet, Ronald Duncan.

population and whole villages disappeared. Labour became in great demand, villagers moved further afield to offer their services or set themselves up independently, and a new class of successful farmers, merchants and tradesmen was born. As noblemen were building great houses all over the South-East and gradually spreading North (and noblewomen too, like Bess of Hardwick who built 'Hardwick Hall, more glass than wall', in Elizabethan times), so the new 'yeoman' classes were building smaller houses, now referred to as cottages, and it is these which, together with the church, form the hearts of many of our villages today.

The years between 1550 and 1660 are sometimes described as the 'Golden Age' of cottage building, but the ones built in that period were the homes of men of relative means who could afford to use lasting materials. In the past two centuries cottages were built at an ever-increasing rate. Though they look cosy and homely enough now, in his *How the Poor Live*, written in the 1880s, George R. Sims painted a terrible picture of the filth and poverty many of them witnessed:

'The room was no better and no worse than hundreds of its class. It was dirty and dilapidated, with the usual bulging blackened ceiling and the usual crumbling greasy walls. Its furniture was a dilapidated four-post bedstead, a chair, and a deal table. On the bed lay a woman, young, and with features that, before hourly anguish contorted them, had been comely. The woman was dying slowly of heart disease. Death was 'writ large' upon her face. At her breast she held her child, a poor little mite of a baby that was drawing the last drain of life from its mother's breast. The day was a bitterly cold one; through the broken casement the wind came ever and anon in icy gusts, blowing the hanging end of the ragged coverlet upon the bed to and fro like a flag in a breeze.'

The cottages of model villages were built with the best intentions and were a conscious effort to provide better living conditions. Some of the most successful were those built by free churchmen, especially the Quakers. The Cadburys, for example, built the wonderful village of Bournville near Birmingham, which was designed by Alexander Harvey to house workers in the chocolate factory. The shoe-making Clarks of Street in Somerset also built many cottages for their workers and Jordans, near Gerrards Cross in Buckinghamshire, was a settlement built by the Quakers. Their outlook on life went with temperance, and alcohol was not encouraged.

Swindon railway village, with its church and drying ground for clothes lines, has proved itself today, by being ahead of its time and keeping human scale in marked contrast to the factories and offices which dwarf it. William Owen, Lever's company architect, did a good job at the village of Port Sunlight in Cheshire too, as did Lockwood and Mawson at Saltaire in Yorkshire, one of the first industrial model villages. I think my favourite model village of the lot is Whiteley near Cobham in Surrey, built by William Whiteley, the founder of Whiteley's stores in Bayswater, to house retired tradesmen. The village is carefully landscaped and provides seemingly casual vistas, churches, chapels, communal halls and comfortable homes. (William Whiteley was shot by his illegitimate son.) Of the private estate villages, I think the most beautiful is the most famous, Milton Abbas in Dorset. It was designed in the 1770s possibly by Sir William Chambers, and blends naturally with the landscape.

Garden suburbs are quite distinct from garden cities. Garden suburbs came first, and the pioneer Arts and Crafts garden suburb was Norman Shaw's Bedford Park, Middlesex. A ballad of the time said of these houses:

'With red and blue and sagest green
Were walls and dado dyed,
Friezes of Morris' there were seen
And oaken wainscot wide.
Now he who loves aesthetic cheer
And does not mind the damp
May come and read Rossetti here
By a Japanese-y lamp.'

Dame Henrietta Barnett was the daughter of a clergyman, who lived first in Whitechapel and then moved with her husband to Hampstead where she founded one of the first garden suburbs. She wanted to bring sunlight and nature into the lives of the poor. Every

EYE, SUFFOLK

Suffolk used to be one of the most densely populated counties in England and one of the most prosperous during the dizzy heights of the wool trade in the 15th and 16th centuries, and it saw the building of many a great church and village. In the 1850s Suffolk's population began to dwindle and during the great agricultural slump of the 1880s it dwindled still further. There remain five or six hundred moated farmsteads with soaring chimney stacks – reminders of former wealth – many of which have become humble cottages such as this one, standing in the flat, drained fields of Constable country.

home in the Suburb is so arranged that it can be seen to be as good at the back as it is at the front. In fact it was the reverse of façadism. Towns had grown straight and packed along streets, but the garden suburb brought nature in-between, fresh air from the Hampstead hills and a village atmosphere. Letchworth and Welwyn garden cities were thought of as communities with a life of their own,

As state rooms in the great houses of England were designed for walking in and the furniture was to be seen in three dimensions, so Picturesque cottages were to be seen as three-dimensional pictures from a window across the park. They were also built to be walked round and gazed at. Perhaps the best example of all is Blaise Hamlet for it is not only a pleasure to walk round but provides a new view with every step you take. Harford's old retainers who moved in to its cottages in 1812 were actually comfortable; many former inhabitants of picturesque cottages had been living in the pitch dark under exaggerated eaves and behind windows of heavily leaded lights. In the park of Alton Towers, Uttoxeter, in Nottinghamshire, Loudon created perhaps the oddest picturesque folly of all which looked like Stonehenge built in two storeys, and near it there was a pagoda which alternately spurted out gas-light and water.

Arts and Crafts cottages were the last rumble of a farm cart in an uneven country lane. The estate cottages at Buscot and Eaton Hastings in Berkshire built by the Butler-Henderson family are a perfect example. The Butler-Hendersons financed a railway company, the beginning of which was the Manchester, Sheffield and Lincolnshire line, soon known as the 'M S and L' ('Money Sunk and Lost'); it then became the Great Central Railway or 'G C' ('Gone Completely'). Despite losing a lot of money they built numerous stone cottages designed by Sir Ernest George. During the last war they were inhabited by Basque refugees at the invitation of Lord Faringdon and became known as the Basque Cottages. They are a lasting tribute to the influence of William Morris, lying across the Thames in Kelmscott churchyard under a stone designed by Philip Webb, whom Norman Shaw described as 'a very interesting man with a strong liking for the ugly'.

Ugly the cottages in this book certainly are not. Is this why we love them so? I do not think it is for their beauty alone. People much prefer things hand done. For the last two

WISBECH, CAMBRIDGESHIRE

This once lonely and remote farm labourer's cottage standing in what Defoe described as the 'base, unwholesome air' of the Fen country around Wisbech is now dwarfed to Lilliputian dimensions by some of the largest corn driers in the land, which tower into the wide sky a hundred yards away. In the 17th century Cambridgeshire's natural commodities were eels, hares, saffron and willows. Its manufactures were paper and baskets and its great wonder the 'Devil's Ditch', a huge dyke striding across the Fens. Well into Victorian times many a moonlighting farm labourer supplemented his income by catching eels and hares, and weaving baskets with withies.

centuries people who did not have to live in cottages have been irresistibly attracted by them, sometimes to the point of obsession. In 1906 G. L. Morris and E. Wood wrote, in their book *The Country Cottage*, something which is as apt today as it would have been at the end of the 18th century:

> 'The increasing demand for "a cottage in the country" is not confined to any one class of people, nor is it any longer significant of a humble mode of life. In olden days the dwellers in cottages were presumably the poor. Poets hymned the cottager as the man of toil, to whom the kindly parson ministered at his family festivals, and for whom the joy of living must depend largely on his relations with the squire. The cottage lass went barefoot from poverty rather than from choice, and her kindred accepted the hewing of wood and the drawing of water as the chief of the inevitable duties of life ... Cottages are wanted to suit almost every kind of domestic life that can be found in English society. The home of one of our younger princesses of the royal blood is a cottage of much smaller dimensions than the house of many a prosperous tradesman. Its elegance lies in what it fulfils of that simplicity and frugality of life – so much easier to conceive than to live up to – which seem to be the last word of a true civilisation.'

The last sentence is, I think, what we are after – 'the simplicity and frugality of life'; but how uncomfortable and sometimes how pretentious some of us have been in that search.

As early as the 1780s people who *certainly* did not need to do so were already living in cottages. Richard Payne Knight, a well-known theorist of the Picturesque movement, relinquished his large and fanciful Downton Castle in Shropshire with its marble dining-room inspired by the Pantheon and its army of servants, and retired to a small cottage on his estate. He referred to it as 'my little domestic dell', and scorned his peers for spending their time 'pent up in a bed or a dining room or ... toiling through turnip fields and stubble in pursuit of partridges'. He went on in a letter to his friend, Lord Aberdeen, 'They really do not know what a delightful planet this is, or what a delicious portion of it has fallen to the lot of us grumbling Englishmen'.

There was a certain smugness about those Picturesque theorists, who, though they

STEEL RIGG, PEEL, HENSHAW, NORTHUMBERLAND

A 19th-century hind's cottage close to Hadrian's Wall. In Northumberland there was a large class of female farm workers, known as bondagers, who were the servants of the hind, who in turn was the farmer's servant. The bondagers were always unmarried, aged between ten and thirty, and they would live in. On the larger farms there might be six or eight hinds, each with two or three bondagers to help him. They would work in gangs, chiefly out of doors, but if there was little to do on the land, bondagers were not bound, like other women, to take on trivial household tasks. Instead they would be allowed to lounge about like lads 'and whistle or snooze' until they were ordered afield.

eulogized the glories of cottage life, did not know true poverty or anything near it, and I wonder if they spent most of their time writing of sublimity from the comfort of their libraries? The writers, however, were probably the most genuine 'new' cottage dwellers of that period. In the early 1800s William and Dorothy Wordsworth, and later Mary, found true happiness in their Lakeland home Dove Cottage.

> 'Yes, Mary, to some lowly door
> In that delicious spot obscure
> Our happy feet shall tend.'

Thomas de Quincey took on Dove Cottage after the Wordsworths and remained in it for twenty-six years, living, it seems, in comfort:

> 'Candles at 4 o'clock, warm hearth rugs, tea, a fair tea-maker, shutters closed, curtains flowing in ample draperies on the floor whilst the wind and the rain are raging without.'

Eventually the number of his children and books became so many that he was obliged to leave for a larger house.

The vogue for the 'simple life' took off and flourished over the first few decades of the 19th century. The rich began to settle in the country, especially beside the sea, in elegant cottages. In his *Life in the English Country House* (1978), Mark Girouard describes:

> 'The strong element of artificiality in the whole back-to-nature movement came into the open in one of its most engaging but also ridiculous products, the *cottage orné* – the simple life, lived in simple luxury in a simple cottage with – quite often – fifteen simple bedrooms, all hung with French wallpapers.'

Though Regency society took the idea of the cottage far beyond its limits, the desire for a little place in the country burned fervently and more genuinely through the second half of the 19th century. The English fondness for the rustic was epitomized by Helen Allingham and Birket Foster's watercolours of idyllic rose-covered cottages, many of which were in Surrey and Sussex. Surrey had been the least populated of the home

BRAINTREE, ESSEX

Plaster has been used as a wall covering in England for over a thousand years and is a familiar sight in Essex where clay was always plentiful. The earliest methods of mixing plaster involved softening the clay with cow hair and dung to make it easier to spread over the walls. It was then lime-washed for extra protection. The cloth industry in this part of England was still booming in the 18th century, and Essex farmers, who would have lived in cottages such as this, could find no female labour of any kind – all the women and girls in rural areas flocked to Braintree and Bocking, Sudbury and Coggeshall, where they could earn far more than the twelve pence a week offered for working on the land.

counties, being wild and difficult to get to, but in the 1850s the railway opened its glories to the cottage builder and dweller. Once again, it was the artistically inclined who led the way into the gay gardens of the home counties.

> 'Bring orchids, bring the foxglove spire,
> The little speedwell's darling blue,
> Deep tulips dash'd with fiery dew
> Laburnums, dropping-wells of fire.'

wrote Tennyson who lived for over twenty years in a house on Leith Hill called Aldworth, in Sussex just over the Surrey borders.

William Morris, poet, craftsman and socialist, revived the simple life in many a middle-class heart. Colonies of 'new' cottagers began to spring up all over the place, and gained momentum by the 1900s. Artists and artisans like the group at Sapperton in Gloucestershire set other shining examples. Writers, poets and film-makers clustered round Clough Williams-Ellis's Portmeirion in North Wales in whitewashed cottages on verdant mountain-sides.

In the 1920s, it became very much 'the thing' to have a cottage in the country – actors and actresses had them tucked away in Kent. People put up with any discomfort provided it was the country. You could buy cottages for £200–£300 then. Nowadays the desire for a thatched half-timbered cottage dripping with honeysuckle is almost universal. Estate agents echo the advertisements in the pattern books of the 1800s:

> 'Perfectly restored and modernised period cottage affording much charm and character and many exposed timbers, within easy reach of Etchingham Station.'

(How amazed Cobbett would have been to see the hovels he visited, bedecked with bathrooms and with a Jaguar parked outside.)

I would like to say how grateful I am to my daughter for sharing my pleasure in looking at buildings. The great thing is not to bore, and 'one good illustration is better than ten pages of text', F. E. Howard used to say. Tony Evans has followed the moods of the book with his excellent photographs.

BRANSDALE, HUTTON-LE-HOLE, YORKSHIRE

A farm labourer's cottage set at the remote head of Bransdale which is often cut off from the world in winter. It was not only men who worked on the land – women also did their fair share. The scholar A. J. Munby wrote in 1862 of Yorkshire: 'a woman all alone, diligently plying her hoe; cleaning out the hedge bottom, one would say. A nice looking young married woman she was, with light hair and sun-burned face; wearing a crumpled bonnet, a tattered cotton frock, and strong earthy boots. She had been working there by herself all day . . . stubbing wickwood and hoeing . . . had worked afield all her life, woman and wench: hoeing, digging taters, harvesting.'

I f you travel from the fertile valleys of Somerset to the watery marshes of Lincolnshire, from a Sussex downland village like West Dean to a wild moorland one like Sparrowpit in Derbyshire, you will see greater variation of building styles and materials in shorter distances than anywhere else in the world, for England is one of the most geologically complicated countries known to man. At one moment in West Hanney in Berkshire you find brick and half-timbered cottages, and the next moment, two miles away in the village of Lyford, you are amidst buff-coloured stone. Northumberland and Northamptonshire, Hampshire and Nottinghamshire are like separate countries – worlds apart – and this is not just because the lie of the land is different, but because the people, their needs and their local building materials were different, and their buildings evolved to suit all three. The soft white clunch cottages of Uffington clustering round one of the best churches in England are as different from the great granite blocks which make the cottages of Sennen in Cornwall as chalk is from cheese. In a cosy county like Kent where the land was always rich and the oak woods thick, cottages reflect the nature of the land and the people just as the strong, wild spirit of the North is reflected in the square-set, rugged and unadorned cottages of Cumberland.

Cottage builders were limited, until the spread of the Industrial Revolution, by their locality. They built with the nearest and cheapest materials which came to hand – mud in Chittlehampton, timber in Mansell Lacey, flint in Hunworth. To a certain extent, the look of the cottages they built was dictated by their materials; a tree trunk was seldom straight and this was reflected in the lines of a half-timbered cottage; cob walls built up gradually over a year or two were done by eye alone and so their appearance was the effect of chance rather than the result of the exact calculations of today.

Neighbourhoods developed their own styles of building, their own architecture without architects, and because of bad roads and poor communications until well into the 18th century, peculiarities became inherent, fashions were almost unknown, innovations untried and outside influences prevented. As generation succeeded generation, so building traditions were assimilated and passed on. Sidney R. Jones, the master illustrator of village life, wrote in 1912, 'Old workmen still living, can remember the lingering of old traditions; can tell of methods employed, and patterns used, which had

VENTNOR, ISLE OF WIGHT

An early 19th-century farm labourer's cottage near Ventnor built of local malmstone found in the belt of greensand along the south side of the Isle of Wight. Sometimes called 'green Ventnor', this stone was taken as far as Winchester and Chichester to add to the cathedrals' fabric. The steep roof pitch suggests that the cottage was once thatched, and was probably thus in the 1830s when Ventnor was just a small group of cottages. The early Victorians transformed it into the most popular watering place on the Undercliff.

their birth in mediaeval times'. Cottage builders did not merely copy the cottage next door, but gave each an individual stamp. A collection of cottages in the Cotswolds, say, may be the same in conception, may seem the same from a distance, but each has an individuality which distinguishes it from the next because it was built for a specific family, with particular needs, or it may incorporate bits of an earlier cottage.

Until three hundred years ago England was thick with oak forests, making timber the cheapest and most popular building material until it became in short supply in the 17th century, the best timber being saved for building ships. One of the earliest forms of timber structures for cottages was the 'cruck' frame, which was used all over the western side of England. Few examples survive and those that do are mostly in the middle west where stone was not readily on hand to replace out-dated timber-framed cottages. Other early forms of timber structure which survive today in greater numbers are the box frame and the post and truss. The basic structures are supported with extra timbers or 'studs', which are very distinctive to different areas. Cottages in the east of England display 'Kentish studding' or 'close studding' as at West Tarring in Sussex and all over south-east England where timber was very plentiful. The west of England and the Midlands sport square panels which are also still common in Warwickshire, Worcestershire, Herefordshire and Shropshire, Cheshire, Staffordshire and Leicestershire. Villages like Elmley Castle in Worcestershire have a wealth of square-panelled cottages. In the northern counties, though timber-framed cottages are much rarer the main timber uprights are stone based. Timber panels were 'infilled' from the earliest times with wattle and daub, which was often replaced later with brick, or the whole structure covered with rendering or cladding which altogether changed its appearance. With the Agricultural Revolution in the 18th century came an upsurge of enclosures, more efficient equipment for cutting stone, and more brick kilns, all of which led to the disappearance of literally thousands and thousands of timber-framed cottages to make way for the more durable qualities of stone and brick. It is difficult to date half-timbered cottages, and owners almost invariably tell you that their cottage dates back to the 15th century. In the case of small cottages this is unlikely to be true. On the whole half-timbered cottages *look* much older than they are on account of wonky timber and the re-use of old materials.

Along with timber, unbaked earth, like cob, clay, wychert, mud and turf, was one of the earliest building materials and commonly used all over the country. Because it disintegrates rapidly unless well cared for there is little left, again except in areas where stone was scarce or too hard to work. Cob has been much the greatest survivor and, combined with thatch, it completes the 'olde worlde' look of villages like Dunsford, Lustleigh, Clovelly and Appledore in Devon, Selworthy and Luccombe in Somerset, and Kilkhampton in Cornwall, which are seldom left off calendars or left alone by tourists. In East Anglia clay lump was widely used and made into unbaked bricks or 'bats' from yellow clay and straw; Shipdham in Norfolk is rich in it. Wychert, a rare clay-like substance found just below the surface, is found most famously in a six-mile radius of Haddenham in Buckinghamshire, some of whose cottages are built in it.

Although stone was plentiful in some shape or form from pebbles to granite, it was only used in a crude way until the 17th and 18th centuries, when stone-cutting saws made it more easily available to cottage builders. There is no doubt that stone is England's finest and noblest building material, and was already accepted as such by the builders of great houses from the 17th century onwards. England's stone is dominated by the magnificent limestone belt which sweeps upwards from Purbeck in the South-West across England to Yorkshire in the North-West, and has produced quarries such as Portland, Doulting and Bath, Barnack, Clipsham, Collyweston and unequalled villages in Dorset, Somerset, Wiltshire, Gloucestershire, Oxfordshire, Northamptonshire, Rutland, Lincolnshire, Leicestershire and Yorkshire. The Cotswolds are perhaps the most loved limestone area and the cottages of Bibury, the Bourtons and the Barringtons, of Snowshill, the Slaughters and the Swells seem literally to be growing out of the landscape along with the sheep and dry stone walls which enclose them. (Upper and Lower Slaughter were once Upper and Lower Mary's Laughter.) The colour of limestone changes gloriously from the pale buff cottages of Little Bredy near the sea in Dorset to the rich dark gold 'ironstone' cottages straddling the steep streets of Rockingham in Northamptonshire, and from the soft gold of the Windrush Valley to the hard blue-grey of the Pennines.

Sandstone appears in the South-West, but as a cottage building material mainly in the North-West. It looks particularly well in Cumberland and Westmorland where its colours range from the palest of pink in the park of Dalemain House near Lake Ullswater through brown to autumnal red in Kirkoswald. Granite, the hardest of all English stone, was used in isolated pockets in Cornwall, whose cottages on the green at Blisland bordering Bodmin Moor must be some of the finest examples of granite building, and also in Westmorland, Cumberland and Northumberland. In the chalk and flint belts which run from Dorset to East Anglia and from Dorset to Sussex, both materials were used for want of a greater stone. Chalk, the softest of stones, needs brick or a harder stone to protect its edges. Flint and pebbles were extremely fiddly to build with but worth the trouble, for where would we be without the chequered cottages of Teffont Magna, the stripy cottages of Nether Cerne, the downland flint cottages of Aldworth in Berkshire, of Droxford in Hampshire, of East Dean, Cocking and Firle in Sussex, the beach pebble cottages of Aldeburgh in Suffolk and, to crown them all, the flint and pebble cottages of Norfolk – Cley-next-the-Sea, Wiveton, Blakeney, Morston, Stiffkey and so on?

Brick kilns proliferated in Queen Elizabeth I's prosperous reign, and bricks gradually became cheap enough to be used by the cottage builder in the last quarter of the 17th century. Brick was widely used throughout the areas where timber-framed cottages predominated, all over the eastern side of England and from the Midlands across to County Durham. The South-West remained content with cob and stone, the limestone belters and the North-West with stone. Before the advent of uniform mass-produced bricks, the colour and tone of bricks varied widely – even when they came from the same kilns. The colour depended on the iron content in the local clay, the firing process and the fuel used to fire the kilns. Bricks emerged richest red in the Weald of Kent, rosiest red in villages like Marston in Lincolnshire, brightest red in the Midlands, particularly in Cheshire, Staffordshire and Worcestershire, and a relentless red in Lancashire, some of whose bricks were known as 'Accrington Bloods'. 'White bricks' (called 'white Cosseys' round Norwich) are in fact pale yellow and were used to make cottage walls in the Soke of Peterborough, the Isle of Ely, Huntingdonshire, Norfolk, Suffolk and most particularly in villages around Cambridge. London produced yellowy brown bricks called 'stocks' and brown bricks swept the Vale of York as in cottages at Bishop Wilton. South Oxfordshire and Berkshire bricks called 'grizzles' displayed different ranges of a

SMARDEN, ASHFORD, KENT

Kent, once thick with oak woods and always rich in farmland, was one of the earliest counties in England to be tamed, and many of its villages date back to the 14th century. This group, near Smarden, is a characteristic example of what we now call cottages, but which were in their time the homes of top-drawer villagers. The cottage on the left, later divided into two, housed the three chaplains to the Church of St Michael's in Smarden, where a chantry was founded in 1392, and it is now called The Brothers. The cottage on the right was the home of a 17th-century clock-maker and the middle part was added a century later.

WALSHAM-LE-WILLOWS, IXWORTH, SUFFOLK

Walsham-le-Willows is an oasis of a village set among enormous prairie fields. It has always depended on the land and good husbandry, and, having been missed by the railway in the 19th century, has not been much affected by commercial industry nor been invaded as a dormitory for Bury St Edmunds. Since the 17th century, when it was built, this cottage has seen little radical change but for the replacement of the thatched roof, probably in the last century, by pantiles which are more or less peculiar to Eastern England. The cottage is painted regularly every two years and, as William Morris advocated, has had constant care and maintenance, a little bit at a time, rather than a complete going over at any one time.

wonderful purplish grey best seen on cottages in Wallingford and Harewell in Berkshire as well as at Cuxham and Nettlebed in Oxfordshire. Different areas had different ways of laying bricks, the most usual of which was 'English Bond' ('headers' lying through the depth of the wall and 'stretchers' lying the length). Other methods included 'Flemish Bond', 'English Garden Wall', 'Yorkshire Bond' and 'Rat Trap'.

Surface materials were added to old, and sometimes new cottages, as a precaution against fire, as a guardian against the elements, for status, and, most particularly in the South-East, to protect timber frames. Weatherboarding in villages like Smarden and Tenterden in Kent and Leigh-on-Sea in Essex gave cottages a clean-cut Georgian look when in fact it often covered earlier irregularly shaped cottages. Plain and mathematical tile hanging was also usual in the South-East; it was considered superior to weatherboarding, and often used for effect rather than genuine necessity. Groombridge in Kent, and Ditchling Common in Sussex show good examples. Slate hanging was an obvious weather combatant against the salty air on Cornish and other coastal cottages and rendering with roughcast or pebble-dash was common in the north of England to keep out the draughts. Plaster, the most ancient of all wall coverings, has been used in England for over a thousand years. It is seen at its best, sometimes decorated with 'pargeting', in Suffolk, Essex, Hertfordshire and Cambridgeshire, topped incidentally with the finest brick chimneys in the country.

The final and necessary touch in most people's minds to the ideally picturesque cottage is thatch. It was once the most common roofing material on all cottages from Yorkshire southwards – it was cheap and, when properly looked after, gave good protection. In fact it was so universal that the dialect word 'thack' is still used to describe any roofing material. However, the 18th century saw a roofing revolution and much of England's thatch was replaced with Welsh slates, plain tiles and pantiles. If you see a tiled or slated roof with a steep pitch it often indicates that the cottage was originally thatched. There are only fifty thousand thatched cottages left in England, which is not very many to go round.

The beginning of the Agricultural Revolution in the 1760s brought the beginning of the end to local styles and materials. Until then villages had grown out of their surroundings as naturally as oaks and elms. Gradually better roads and new canals made it possible to transport materials with comparative ease. Bath stone sailed up navigation channels to villages which had never seen it before, bricks from local kilns were trundled on carts to remote hamlets. The introduction of cottage pattern books in the 1770s, which became very numerous by the 1830s, meant that local craftsmen – masons, carpenters and thatchers – were able to see how others built in different parts of the country. New styles were tried, new fashions attempted, new tricks of the trade adopted. So building became less and less localized and materials like brick more, and eventually completely, universal. In 1842 the introduction of the blueprint made it possible to reproduce buildings *en masse*; until then it had been up to the builder himself to interpret the design in a pattern book. Skilled craftsmen were no longer needed on site, they became less in demand and unskilled labour took over. In isolated cases, local styles and materials were still adhered to, particularly on great estates where the extra money and effort involved was not important (and the Arts and Crafts movement advocated a return to them), but it was a conscious form of building and meant the end of true unconscious local building.

From time immemorial, from the timber tent-like structures which clustered round the church and manor of mediaeval villages to the socially conscious living quarters of Milton Keynes under its orange night sky, the needs of man have remained unchanged – a place to shelter, eat and sleep. Then, each dwelling was individual, each area familiar through its styles and materials; now each dwelling seems a replica of the one next door, and many areas indistinguishable from one another. Drop blindfold into any new housing estate in England and you would not know whether you were in Cornwall or Cumberland. Drop blindfold into the heart of any of our villages and you would know the county (except that, for some inexplicable reason, its name might have been changed).

DIDBROOK, STANWAY, GLOUCESTERSHIRE

Until the 17th century woodland covered much of the English countryside and timber, preferably oak, was the most popular building material. The earlier the building, the more the timber imposed its architectural form. Cruck Cottage displays the most basic of structural systems – the 'cruck frame' – an adaptation of the tent structure of the most primitive huts. Leaving the exact breadth for a team of oxen, four abreast, between them, two curving poles or 'crucks' were stuck in the ground and leaned towards each other to support a ridge pole. Another pair of crucks was then set sixteen feet away, the distance required to stable two teams of oxen. (This functional unit of measurement has survived for room sizes to this day.) Additional bays could easily be added later and the bases of the crucks were usually supported in stone or brick. Often the Lord of the Manor would donate a tree for the first pair of crucks. These took a chevron form and became a symbol of favour or position; they still persist today in an inverted form on the sleeves of non-commissioned officers and policemen, etc. The merit of the cruck frame was its extreme simplicity and it is still used today in the construction of smaller houses, and referred to as the 'A' frame.

31

EARDISLAND,
LEOMINSTER,
HEREFORDSHIRE

Another early form of timber
construction was the 'box frame',
in which pairs of posts supported
cross beams. The building would
start as an open box of timber
which was then sub-divided by
vertical and horizontal pieces
pegged together with wooden
pegs to make a frame of squares
which could then be infilled with
a suitable material. Ruscote was
built in the early 17th century by
a native of the county, John Abel.
It was re-thatched in 1972 by Mr
Jones of Onibury in Shropshire.

COUGHTON, ALCESTER,
WARWICKSHIRE

Until the advent of electricity and
motor cars nearly every village
had its forge which was situated
at the heart of things. The
blacksmith's cottage was usually
attached to the shop itself – as was
this cottage at Coughton. The
blacksmith was indispensable for
not only was he farrier and
sometimes horse vet, but also he
supplied everything made of iron
from farm machinery to tailor's
scissors.

'Week in, week out, from morn till nig
  You can hear his bellows blow;
  You can hear him swing his heavy sle
  With measured beat and slow,
  Like a sexton ringing the village bell,
  When the evening sun is low.'
H.W. Longfe
The Village Blacks

ABBOTS MORTON,
INKBERROW,
WORCESTERSHIRE

Black and white cottages are a
common sight in the apple
orchard county of
Worcestershire. Because stone
was not prolific in the Midlands,
many early half-timbered
cottages have survived here,
whereas in other parts of
England they were often replaced
with the more enduring qualities
of stone. Corner Thatch was built
as a barn in the 18th century, was
later converted into a cottage and
until recently was the local post
office in the small and almost
perfect Worcestershire village of
Abbots Morton. Generally you
can judge the age of a timber-
framed building by the closeness
and thickness of the timbers. The
later the cottage the more
sparsely the timber was used.

RAMSBURY,
MARLBOROUGH,
WILTSHIRE

Rose Cottage is in the middle of
the predominantly brick village
of Ramsbury near to the Downs.
Part of the charm of 'olde worlde'
cottages is the complete absence
of gutters and down pipes. They
are not necessary, but a steep roof
pitch is essential to ensure that
rain-water is quickly thrown off
and does not have time to sink in.
This late 16th-century cottage,
complete with a 'catslide'
extension of the main roof to
cover an outhouse, has been in
Mrs Puffett's family for nearly a
hundred years. Her father was a
gardener at Ramsbury Manor
and her husband has worked with
racehorses for most of his life.

BELLS YEW GREEN,
BAYHAM, SUSSEX

This cottage is thatched in
heather (which was not unusual
in Sussex) and has reed thatch
from the Romney Marshes laid
on top. Originally the home of a
tinker, it is half-timbered with
wattle and daub infill beneath. It
was weatherboarded around 1870
when it became the home of a
gamekeeper and known as The
Pheasantry. The windows were
probably enlarged at this time.

'If I ever become a rich man
Or if ever I grow to be old,
I will build a house with deep thatch
To shelter me from the cold,
And there shall the Sussex songs be sung
And the story of Sussex told.'
Hilaire Belloc

TROW, SALCOMBE REGIS,
DEVONSHIRE

By about 1200 thatching was no
longer used on houses of any
stature, but continued to be a
common roofing material on
more humble homes well into the
18th century. Since thatch only
lasts for about a hundred years, it
is difficult to assess its history,
but certainly the most usual
thatching materials have long
been reed, straw and heather.
Because it was the lightest form
of roofing it was widely used in
areas like Devon, where wall
structures were weak.

GITTISHAM, HONITON, DEVONSHIRE

The warm moist climate of Devon causes cottage gardens to flourish, and at Gorse Cottage in Gittisham roses romp up the walls as they have done traditionally for centuries. Miss Mitford described in *Our Village* in the middle of the last century, 'The walls . . . covered with hollyhocks, roses, honeysuckles . . . the casements full of geraniums . . . and the little garden full of common flowers, tulips, pinks, larkspurs, peonies, stocks and carnations with an arbour of privet, not unlike a sentry-box, where one lives in a delicious green light, and looks on the gayest of all flower-beds.'

ULLCOMBE, HONITON, DEVONSHIRE

Originally part of Lord Sidmouth's estate, this early 17th-century cottage has been lived in by the Blackmore family for over a hundred years. The cottage was re-thatched in 1978 at a cost of £3,000 and was re-ridged in 1981 at a cost of £400. In his *The Compleat Builders Guide*, published in 1726, Neve says that 'Common Thatch is done in some places for 2/6 per square [100 sq. ft.] and for Thatching with Reed they have 4/– per square. A Thatcher of my Acquaintance tells me that one Rubble Mason . . . proffer'd (for a small matter) to teach him how to Thatch a Roof so, that no Mouse nor Rat should come into it: But he was not so thoughtful then, as to get the Receipt of him, tho' it would have been of no small use to him; for the Rubble Mason said, he knew a Thatcher that had 4d per square more for doing it so. It is a thing worth inquiring after.'

UPOTTERY, DEVONSHIRE

Whitehall Cottage is built of cob, a word used to describe unbaked earth in the south-west of England. Cob is a carefully blended mixture of wet earth, (containing enough lime to enable it to set), chopped reed, straw or animal dung, sand, gravel and small stones as balast. The Devon saying, 'All cob wants is a good hat and a good pair of shoes' means that all cob needs is a good roof and a good plinth. So long as cob keeps dry it will last for centuries, but if the rain gets to it it will disintegrate rapidly. This late 16th-century cottage has a stone plinth which was built not only to keep the cob dry but also to keep out rats and other vermin.

HARPFORD, NEWTON POPPLEFORD, DEVONSHIRE

Approached by deep fern-banked lanes, Little Thatch (one-up-and-one-down) nestles cosily in the village of Harpford by the River Otter. It has a neat thatched porch with barley-sugar columns and a steep 'catslide' roof at the back shielding what could have been a water closet at the beginning of this century. Writing in the 1830s John Loudon, the landscape architect, had said that no cottage was complete without one 'under the same roof, or under a lean-to. The well or tanks for liquid manure connected with it are as advantageous, in point of profit, to every cottager who has a garden, as the water closet or privy itself is essential to cleanliness and decency.' Very few people took any notice of this hopeful statement, and even new cottages were not necessarily equipped with a simple earth closet until the late 19th century.

BRANSCOMBE, SEATON, DEVONSHIRE

A cob cottage overlooking beautiful Branscombe Church set in a sheltered valley leading to the sea. The buttresses either side of the door have been added to give extra support to the bulging cob. Cob walls, seldom less than two and sometimes four feet thick, were built up in layers about six to twelve inches high, and each layer had to set before another was added. In bad weather things would come to a standstill and a two-storey cottage could take up to two years to build. The building up of the cob (called clob in Cornwall) was done by eye alone and accounts for the rounded and undulating look of some cob walls.

STINSFORD, DORCHESTER, DORSET

The finishing touch to a cob wall is a coat of lime-plaster rendering and a regular coat of colour, whitewash or tar, which was meant to deter cattle from licking holes in the walls. This freshly whitewashed pair of cottages is in Stinsford, the original of Thomas Hardy's Mellstock. Hardy's grandfather was the cello player in Stinsford Choir, and together with other church instrumentalists was perpetuated in Melstock Quire. The heart of Thomas Hardy was buried in Stinsford Church in 1928 and the general feeling among local people was that the division of the body for a separate burial in Westminster Abbey was sacrilegious. A local inhabitant, Miss Dorothy Meggison, recalls hearing an elderly Stinsford woman saying, 'and when Day of Judgment be come, Almighty, 'E'll say: "'Ere be 'eart, but where be the rest of 'e?"'

UPOTTERY, DEVONSHIRE

Mrs Witt's cob cottage has been in her family for over three generations. Her grandfather, Northcote Robins, who was born in 1830, was a builder and in his day Church Cottage extended to the right of the picture and incorporated his carpenter's workshop as well as a sweet shop. When he died in 1901 these were demolished and the land was given to the churchyard. Carpenters in Northcote Robins's time had to be for ever on the lookout for work: 'It was a sort of grapevine, it used to go all round . . . "big job coming out so and so" – you used to keep your eye on that job – say you were working somewhere else (you'd think), "Well that'll be ready about so and so" – see – well, if your job petered out you'd be round . . .' (From *Village Life and Labour*, 1975).

LITTLE BREDY, DORCHESTER, DORSET

Through Dorset a great swathe of limestone sweeps upwards through England, from Purbeck on the coast across the Cotswolds and up to Yorkshire and beyond. This row of thatched cottages in pale Dorset limestone was once known as Widows' Walk, and traditionally housed the widows of the village under the auspices of the local Lord of the Manor. It has since been renamed Church Walk, after a widow or two were whisked up the aisle.

UFFINGTON, FARINGDON, BERKSHIRE

Much of the village of Uffington at the foot of White Horse Hill is built of 'clunch' – a form of chalk pebble found either on or just below the surface of the surrounding land. In comparison with other stone it is soft and easy to work, but disintegrates if exposed to damp, frost or smoky atmospheres. Cottages were usually built on a stone base with brick, flint or limestone dressings to protect exposed areas like window-sills. Sally Weaver was born in Pear Tree Cottage in 1941 and was married from it when she was sixteen. There was a thunderstorm in the morning and the present poet laureate wrote in his poem *Sally Weaver's Wedding*:

'The chalk white walls, the steaming thatch
In rainwashed air are clearing,
And waves of sunshine run to catch
The bride for her appearing.'

ALTON PRIORS, PEWSEY, WILTSHIRE

This simple stone farm labourer's cottage looks much as it would have looked when it was built in 1831, with its meandering approach across the village green. Mr Wiltshire, who lives here, has worked on the local farm for forty-nine years and can remember when there were thirty or more shire horses on the place. Until the 1900s farm labourers did not necessarily stick to one particular trade and a general change-about of places happened every year or half year. A hay trusser might turn thatcher after the summer and present himself at one of the local Michaelmas hiring fairs, such as the Mop in Marlborough, where there were stalls and merry-go-rounds and where heavy drinking took place. Men, women and children were bid for by farmers like beasts at a cattle market. Fairs did not always take place in large towns but often in isolated places such as Tan Hill, a few miles from Alton Priors. This fair attracted people from all over the south-west of England, and was an occasion for exchanging news, views and ideas, and wheeling and dealing and general social diversion until as recently as the early 1900s.

STANWAY, WINCHCOMBE, GLOUCESTERSHIRE

Originally two dwellings, The Old Thatch was completely derelict twenty years ago, but has been lovingly restored by its present owners. The topiary bird of yew has long been a traditional part of the English cottage garden. The fashion for formal topiary gardens began in England in the 16th century, was sported at Hampton Court and grew in popularity through the 17th century. Cottage gardeners imitated the big house up the road by displaying their craftsmanship in a single piece of topiary; when the landscaped gardens of the 18th century swept away topiaries by the thousand, cottagers clung religiously to their peacocks and pyramids and have done so to this day.

AVEBURY, WILTSHIRE

Cottages built within the Avebury Circle, one of the greatest megalithic monuments in the world. In the 18th century local builders found a way to break up the Great Stones by lighting fires around them and then throwing cold water on them while they were very hot. Many of the Great Stones which formed the inner circle and the long avenue which led towards it, were thus broken up and used to build the village of Avebury, including these cottages.

BIBURY,
GLOUCESTERSHIRE

Arlington Row was built in 1360
by the Augustinian friars as a
wool store and converted into
cottages in the 17th century to
house weavers supplying cloth to
the nearby Arlington Mill. The
wool fleece was converted into
yarn in the workers' homes and
then woven on a hand loom.
When in full employment,
weavers, according to the Rev.
J. Wilkinson in an article in the
Wiltshire *Archaeological
Magazine* in 1860, were '14 hours
a day at it, hands, arms, legs and
feet in full play'. Sometimes
before weaving and sometimes
after, the cloth was scoured by
dyers or fullers using stale urine,
which was collected from local
public houses or receptacles
placed at street corners, its
collector being called 'piss
Harry'. One of the last processes
in the production of cloth was
'tentering' or stretching it on
tenterhooks, hence the well-
known phrase.

BADMINTON, SODBURY,
GLOUCESTERSHIRE

No. 5 Jockey Row is part of a row
of cottages renovated towards the
end of the 19th century by the
Badminton Estate to incorporate
dormer windows with elegant
barge-boards, typical of that date.
Bob Knott, who lives here, still
sleeps in the room he was born in
seventy-six years ago, and has
been a gardener at Badminton
House for fifty years. His father
walked into the cottage a hundred
years ago when he was married.

NOTGROVE,
NORTH LEACH,
GLOUCESTERSHIRE

Two of the main factors which made Cotswold cottages perhaps a cut above the rest from the 17th century onwards were a constant supply of good limestone, and prosperity from the sheep which grazed in their thousands on the rolling hills. One of the most characteristic Cotswold features, as on this cottage at Notgrove, are the dormer windows built to form gables in the stone-flagged roof. Limestone is comparatively soft and easy to work, which accounts for the other distinctive details of Cotswold cottages, such as cleanly moulded drip stones and mullions. Everything from the chimneys to the garden paths to the field walls was built in the same coloured stone, whose mellow tones have captivated many a coachload of enthusiasts from Ilkley to Illinois.

SAPPERTON,
CIRENCESTER,
GLOUCESTERSHIRE

No. 21 Sapperton was originally a farmhouse and was built in the 17th century. The pair of cottages on the left were added to house farm labourers; in the 19th century the whole was known in the village as Bachelor's Court since there were three single men living in the three separate dwellings. In 1911 Norman Jewson, who had married the architect Ernest Barnsley's eldest daughter, moved into Bachelor's Court. He converted it into one, skilfully and carefully, with assistance from Sapperton craftsmen and the crafts workshop, founded at nearby Daneway in 1900 by Ernest Barnsley and Ernest Gimson. Norman Jewson's book *By Chance I did Rove* (1950) describes the village of Sapperton and particularly this cottage, his much loved home. His daughter lives here still.

EXTON, OAKHAM, RUTLAND

In soft Rutland country, this simple 18th-century farm labourer's cottage stands in the village of Exton, where stately sycamores circle the green. The accommodation for farm labourers in the 18th century usually consisted of one room with the addition of an out-shut. The whole family slept together, either at one end of the room or in a loft approached by a ladder. The average menu of a farm labourer's family according to Sir Frederick Eden's *The State of the Poor*, published in 1797, consisted of:

'Breakfast: Tea or Bread and cheese.
Dinner and Supper: Bread and cheese, or potatoes, sometimes mashed with fat from broth, and sometimes with salt alone. Bullock's cheek is generally bought every week to make broth. Treacle is used to sweeten tea instead of sugar. Very little milk or beer is used.'

AYNHO, BRACKLEY, NORTHAMPTONSHIRE

Aynho is set on high ground and was once a typical fortified hill village surrounded by a protective wall. A number of ancient cottages survive today, some with outside stairs and many, like this one, have apricot trees growing up their golden yellow walls. The trees were given to the inhabitants by the Lord of the Manor, Squire Cartwright. Cottagers were then asked to pay their tithes in apricots rather than money. The Cartwright family lived through three centuries at Aynho Park from the year 1616.

ASKHAM, HELTON,
WESTMORLAND

The more dramatic the country,
the simpler the architecture of
cottages seems to become. These
cottages, though plain in
themselves, have an air of
independence and seem content
to leave beauty to the scenery of
fell and lakeland. The cottages of
Askham are grouped around a
long green, some with narrow
alleyways between. This was a
method of defence during the
Scottish border raids; when the
village was attacked, livestock
would be driven on to the green
and the small alleyways
barricaded.

PIERCEBRIDGE,
DARLINGTON,
COUNTY DURHAM

It sometimes took fifty years for
the fashions of the South to reach
the North of England and this
late Georgian-looking cottage is
probably 19th-century. The hard
limestones, granites and slates of
the North were difficult to work
and often account for the rugged
look of the cottages. Whitewash
was used not only to protect the
stone but also to soften its
appearance. The decorative lip
mouldings above the windows
and door throw off the rain water.
Once an important Roman
station, Piercebridge straddles
Watling Street on its way from
Dover to Carlisle.

HUTTON-LE-HOLE, YORKSHIRE

Moorside Cottage to the left of the picture was built in 1795 of the local glowing ironstone. In 1900 it was lived in by Mr Pennock Pateman, a taxidermist, and was the first cottage in the village to have a bath installed in the 1930s, causing considerable wonder. It is typical of the more substantial two-bedroomed cottages seen in villages all over Yorkshire.

Nonconformism, particularly Quakerism, was always strong in Hutton-le-Hole, and the Parish Church was not built until the 1930s. Most of the villagers have owned the freeholds of their cottages since the 16th century, as there was no local major landowner. They organized the village through a Manor Court, one of the few that still exist.

HUMSHAUGH, CHOLLERTON, NORTHUMBERLAND

Although by the middle of the 19th century one-storey cottages were considered inferior in the South, they remained widespread in the North of England and were built on a centuries-old pattern, usually with only a single room, and sometimes fitted with built-in box beds. In the 1900s a family with sixteen children lived here, all of whom survived. The sleeping arrangements of the rural poor upset many a Victorian moralist. One of the conditions of a farm servant's tenancy on some estates in Northumberland was that he provide and house a female labourer. Writing about border peasants in 1842 James Cunningham suggested, 'before we can hope to see them chaste, pure or elevated in morals, we must provide them with houses in which propriety and common decency may be observed.'

SIMONBURN, HEXHAM,
NORTHUMBERLAND

Burnside Cottage has been in
Miss Margaret Charlton's family
since the 1880s, and before that
was the birthplace of Edward
Keith who later became the head
gardener at Wallington, one of
the greatest gardens of the North.
Before *his* day it had been the
village school, attended far more
in the winter months than in the
summer when children had to
work on the land. Though girls
did all the jobs that boys did at
home, from turnip-pulling to
manure-spreading, they were not
taught athletics at school like the
boys because it was considered
unsuitable. In 19th-century
Northumberland the authorities
suggested that instead girls
should 'find a little wholesome
physical exercise in cleaning out
the school.'

BLANCHLAND, SLALEY,
NORTHUMBERLAND

Approached in every direction
over wild moorland, the village of
Blanchland was built in the 18th
century by the Earls of Crewe to
house local lead miners. The
village consists of uniformly-built
stone cottages tucked into a
wooded valley near the source of
the Derwent River – 'a frightful
creature when the hills load her
current with water', said Daniel
Defoe in his *A Tour Through The
Whole Island of Great Britain* in
1724. He goes on to describe lead
miners near the Derwent River as
being 'bold, daring and even
desperate kind of fellows in their
search into the bowels of the
earth; for no people in the world
out-do them; and therefore they
are often entertained by our
engineers in the wars to carry on
the sap, and other such works, at
the sieges of strong fortified
places.'

HILLINGTON, KING'S LYNN, NORFOLK

The cottages of Hillington are built of the local Carstone, which is a form of cretaceous sandstone. Although it occurs in occasional pockets in Hampshire and the Isle of Wight, and more often in Bedfordshire, its extraordinary yellow-brown colour is best seen in villages around Snettisham from whence it was quarried. Norfolk people call it 'gingerbread stone' on account of its colouring, which is due to the presence of iron oxide.

LAMBOURN, BERKSHIRE

Originally built as a pair of shepherds' dwellings with a central doorway opening on to two inner doors, this cottage is constructed of sarsen stones ploughed up on the surrounding downs. 'The Downland shepherds were as a rule clever poachers; and it is really not surprising when one considers the temptation to a man with a wife and several hungry children besides himself and a dog to feed out of about 7/– a week.' Caleb's reminiscences, quoted in *A Shepherd's Life*, are contemporary with the time the cottage was built around 1820, when pointed windows were highly fashionable.

LUCCOMBE, MINEHEAD, SOMERSET

In stone building areas, chimney stacks were seldom axial but almost always on the side. Cottage fires were often made of furze or dried animals' dung, and the flames of the fire were generally the only form of light in the evenings, sometimes supplemented by rushlights, which involved a lengthy procedure of dipping rushes in grease. Only the well-off could afford candles. In his *Topographical Dictionary of England*, written in 1842, Samuel Lewis describes the Exmoor village of Luccombe as having 580 inhabitants and being on 'richly fertile soil with the land in a high state of cultivation'.

COOMBE, KILKHAMPTON CORNWALL

Coombe lies deep down a grassy valley on the northernmost tip of the Cornish coast. Its few scattered cottages are now mostly holiday retreats, but in the early 19th century it was where the eccentric Reverend Hawker spent his days, before he became Vicar of nearby Morwenstow. At that time the villagers all around were devoted to smuggling and wrecking, and Hawker did much to reform his parishioners, being much loved and respected. He dressed as a fisherman, invited dogs and cats to his services, wrote poetry and became (and still is) a local legend. It was at Coombe that he wrote the rousing ballad:

'And have they fixed
    the where and when?
And shall Trelawny die?
Here's twenty thousand
    Cornish men
Will know the reason why!'

PORTQUIN, WADEBRIDGE, CORNWALL

This pair of fishermen's cottages built in local slate stands forlorn in the ghost village of Portquin. The Victorian painting by Frank Bramley, *A Hopeless Dawn*, 1888, depicts women in this village who had waited all night for their menfolk to return from fishing after a heavy storm. Their waiting was in vain, for not one man returned, and the village was eventually abandoned at the beginning of this century. Beneath tangled brambles and ivy the remains of several cottages still line the road which winds down the steep dark valley into the cove.

WYLYE, SALISBURY, WILTSHIRE

Walnut Tree Cottage displays chequers of local stone and knapped flint – a common combination of materials in the Wylye Valley. Knapping means splitting a flint in half and making the exposed surface smooth. The use of bands or chequers in areas where flint was abundant was not necessarily for decorative effect, but a way of making the local stone go further. As described in Flora Thompson's *Lark Rise to Candleford* cottage gardens often had a herb corner 'stocked with thyme and parsley and sage for cooking, rosemary to flavour the home-made lard, lavendar to scent the best clothes and peppermint, pennyroyal, horehound, camomile, tansy, balm and rue for physic'.

UPPER WOODFORD, SALISBURY, WILTSHIRE

The chessboard flint and stone cottages of the Woodford Valley, whose villages lie either side of the River Avon, are some of the best in the county. This farm labourer's cottage has been lived in by descendants of the Merrit family for a hundred years. The original Mr Merrit's great-grandson works today on the farm to which the cottage has always belonged. Originally two dwellings, it is fairly typical in size and outline of cottages built in the Regency period. The innovatory close-fitting Welsh roofing slates caught on all over England and enabled fashion-conscious builders to pitch their roofs at a lower angle than before.

HEPWORTH, RICKINGHALL SUPERIOR, SUFFOLK

The use of flint, brick and pantiles is typical in East Anglia. This cottage was built in 1871 when the fashion for pantiles was beginning to decline. Pantiles became a popular roofing material, and a characteristic feature in the east and north-east of England, from the 17th century onwards. The earliest pantiles are found in places which had trading links with Holland, where they originated; and apart from odd pockets in other parts of the country, they were peculiar to the eastern half of England. Their interlocking edges made for less overlap, and therefore fewer tiles and less weight, and 'A great covering of these', says Neve, 'spends but little Mortar and but little Time in laying.'

SIDMOUTH, DEVONSHIRE

The tradition of pebble walling belongs primarily to the north Norfolk coast around Blakeney and Cromer; but there are Regency examples in Brighton and many other resorts of that period such as Sidmouth, where pebbles were used to give character to *cottages ornés*. Pebblestone Cottage, built about 1820, could possibly have been a toll house; but the painstaking arrangements of beach pebbles on the inside as well as the outside walls suggests that it was built as a seaside retreat by some fashionable figure of society.

CLIFTON HAMPDEN, ABINGDON, OXFORDSHIRE

A brick and timber cottage in Clifton Hampden, which boasts many fine examples. During the 'golden age' of cottage building in the 16th and 17th centuries the use of brick spread throughout areas which had formerly been dominated by timber and wattle and daub. After many fires in towns and villages and the Great Fire of London, brick's resistance to fire was an obvious reason for its popularity. In areas where stone was thin on the ground, bricks would be made on the spot providing there was enough clay in the soil. Very often the pits created by digging for clay became the village pond.

HIGHER BOCKHAMPTON, DORCHESTER, DORSET

The birthplace of Thomas Hardy in 1840, this cottage was built by his great grandfather, John Hardy of Puddletown, in 1801, on an uncultivated stretch of land bordering Egdon Heath. Originally of cob, the brick facing was added later and the windows which were leaded lattens have been replaced with wooden casements; but with its thatched roof it still appears much as described in *Under the Greenwood Tree* as Tranter Reuben Dewy's cottage. Hardy's grandfather, an occasional brandy smuggler, built a squint into the front porch to allow him to watch for excise men. Hardy's father was a master builder and the cottage still has a window at the back with iron bars through which he paid his men. Hardy lived here until 1862 when he went to study architecture in London. He returned in 1867 because of ill health and here he wrote *Desperate Remedies*, *Under the Greenwood Tree* and *Far from the Madding Crowd*.

AMPTHILL, BEDFORD, BEDFORDSHIRE

Originally two dwellings, these semi-detached cottages are part of a group of eight. Their date plaques range from 1812 to 1816. The entrance doors were originally in the gable end walls and the chimney stack in the centre. Unless for obvious decorative effect, it is fairly rare to find exposed timber frames of this date, for they would normally be clad. By the second half of the 19th century brick became the universal building material. The brick-making season lasted from April to October, and brick workers often used members of their family to bump up their earnings. Women worked as hard as men, and two villagers, Crowy Kerry and Putt Phillips, remember in the last century Old Mam Wharton who was 'stronger than a lot of the men . . . she used to come up all day and sand the mould and help her husband . . . she was a tough old gal . . . stout, got some go in her. Coorse, they done very well, the two on 'em.'

STAPLEFORD, NOTTINGHAM NOTTINGHAMSHIRE

In the 18th century Leicestershire and Nottinghamshire were the great centres of hosiery, and many stocking frame knitters worked from their homes, which were specially constructed for the purpose. The windows on the top floor where the frames stood admitted as much light as possible. In 1844 there were 16,382 stocking frames in Nottinghamshire, 33 of which were in the village of Stapleford, but by then, because of the introduction of steam power, many of the looms lay idle, and the appearance of the cottages often belied the terrible conditions inside. In 1838 the then oldest Nottinghamshire stocking maker died in his 94th year. The sharp decline of the industry is indicated by the hours he worked – 10 hours a day as a boy, 12 hours a day in middle age and by the end of his life a 16-hour day was scarcely enough for obtaining a bare maintenance. The physical condition of stockingers and their families deteriorated with less and less work and a Nottingham physician said he could easily recognize one in the street: 'There is a paleness and a certain degree of emaciation and thinness about them'. Their diet consisted mainly of bread and cheese, gruel and tea, and infants were often drugged with Godfrey's Cordial.

WHIXALL, WHITCHURCH, SHROPSHIRE

William Jessop, who engineered the Ellesmere Canal in the 1790s, beside which this lock-keeper's cottage stands, was perhaps England's least-lauded canal builder. Although he worked on over twenty major canal and navigation schemes, he was constantly overshadowed by his more famous pupil, Thomas Telford. Jessop did not fancy himself as an architect, and consequently the cottages all along the Ellesmere Canal follow simple local styles. Where the canal had to cross the boggy ground of Whixall Moss, Jessop built up an earth embankment to carry his channel.

WOOL, PURBECK, DORSET

'I covet the idea of being sometimes by myself near a fire with a hope of having a warm solitary place to hide in sometimes on winter evenings,' wrote T. E. Lawrence, or Private Shaw as he then was, to a friend soon after he had found this cottage, Clouds Hill, and rented it in 1923. 'The cottage is alone in a dip in the moor, very quiet, very lonely, very bare. A mile from Camp [Bovington]. Furnished with a bed, a bicycle, three chairs, one hundred books, a gramophone of parts, a table . . . I don't sleep here, but come out at 4.30 p.m.–9 p.m. nearly every evening, and dream, or write, or read by the fire, or play Beethoven and Mozart to myself on the box.' Although T. E. Lawrence left Clouds Hill for long periods he returned whenever he could and finally retired here in 1935. On 8 May of that year he wrote to Lady Astor that wild mares would not persuade him away from his 'earthly paradise', Clouds Hill. Five days later he was fatally injured when his motorbike went out of control while he was swerving to avoid two young boys on bicycles near Clouds Hill.

GREAT LIVERMERE, BURY ST EDMUNDS SUFFOLK

A serpentine reed-banked mere full of heron and other water birds divides Little from Great Livermere, whose beech-shaded cottages are typically Suffolk. Little stone and lots of clay make the county's traditional building materials timber, brick and plaster. This pair of 18th-century cottages are brick and timber beneath plaster for extra protection. They were originally thatched and later roofed with pantiles, which were made locally until the 1900s.

HOXNE, EYE, SUFFOLK

Mulberry Cottage in Hoxne
(pronounced to rhyme with oxen)
is really a 19th-century version of
the true traditional Suffolk style
which has hardly changed since
Tudor times. The barn shape,
steep roof and tall chimneys make
it look like a miniature version of
a grand Tudor house, such as
Thorpe Hall, which stands a few
miles distant across flat fields of
corn.

BENHALL, SAXMUNDHAM, SUFFOLK

Pargeting – the raised or (more
commonly) incised ornamental
design in plaster – is found in
Suffolk and Essex and to a lesser
extent in the surrounding
counties. Most of the original
raised pargeting on this cottage,
built in 1695, would long since
have fallen off with the weight of
constant applications of lime-
wash, so the design has been
picked out in a different colour.

ASKHAM, HELTON, WESTMORLAND

The original core of this cottage is 17th-century, as the low doorway and date plaque of 1674 confirms, but the rest of its appearance can only date from 1870 when cement roughcast, sash windows and machine-cut tiles reached the Lake District. Materials that were weak, like unbaked earth, or rough walls, such as ones made of Silurian and Ordovician stone in the Lake District, were often covered with a surface of roughcast – a mixture of sand, gravel, stone chippings, lime and more lately cement. The addition of too much cement gives a harder, more lasting surface in exchange for a dismal colour and texture.

PLOWDEN, BISHOPS CASTLE SHROPSHIRE

Built of stone quarried at the foot of Long Mynd, four hundred yards away, Park Cottage was later covered in whitewashed roughcast for extra protection. It has been lived in by gamekeepers to the Plowden family for over 150 years, and the present gamekeeper, Mr Pye, has lived here all his life as his father did before him. The area of Park Cottage, Plowden Mill and Plowden Station is the starting point of the Portway, an important trading route linking Wales to the Midlands since Mesolithic times. In the Middle Ages Portway was a famous drovers' route and there would certainly have been dwellings on this site since that time.

PORT ISAAC,
WADEBRIDGE, CORNWALL

The hills of Port Isaac are so
steep and its alleyways so narrow
(Squeezibelly Alley is twenty
inches wide) that donkeys were
used until quite recently to
transport goods to and from the
harbour. Examples of slate-hung
walls as on the 18th-century
Bird Cage Cottage (centre) can be
seen in many a seaside town, but
far more than anywhere in South
Devon and Cornwall. As timber-
framed cottages were unknown in
Cornwall, slates were attached to
rough stone or brick to give extra
protection against the salty air.
The slate quarry at nearby
Delabole has been worked since
1560, and is the largest in
England, being four hundred feet
deep and one mile wide. Celia
Fiennes, who rode side-saddle
through England in 1695, was
impressed by Delabole Hole:
'Remarkable quarries for a black
stone, exceeding hard and glossy
like marble, very durable for
pavements. This they send to all
parts in time of peace, and
London takes much of it.'

82

PADSTOW, CORNWALL

The mediaeval arrangement of having the living quarters on the upper floor still persists in some fishing villages, and doubtless at high spring tides it is a safe place to be. The bottom floor usually had few or no windows and was used for the storage of nets. Local legend has it that there is a subterranean passage from this cottage on the quay to connect it with the monastery which formerly occupied the site of Prideaux Place, a quarter of a mile away. Built into its walls are odd bits of stone tracery which could possibly have come from the monastery.

83

GROOMBRIDGE, TUNBRIDGE WELLS, KENT

The Walks, an 18th-century row of cottages, border one side of the triangular village green in Groombridge – one of the best villages of the Weald. They display tile-hanging on the upper storey and weatherboarding on the lower, and were once towered over by mature chestnut trees, which have recently been replaced. Plain tiles, sometimes slightly thinner than roofing tiles, were used in the south-east of England to cover walls from the end of the 17th century, and were popular throughout the 18th century when hand-made tiles proliferated. Hanging tiles became a speciality in Kent, Sussex and Surrey and were used for cladding cottages well into the 19th century when machine-made tiles made it easier still.

BELLS YEW GREEN, BAYHAM, SUSSEX

Weatherboarding was used in all the home counties, but the earliest examples and the most abundant are in Kent and on the Sussex borders. It is a term used for fixing lengths of board horizontally, usually to an earlier timber-framed building. Its purpose was to give extra warmth and protection. The south-east of England provided many of the early emigrants to America and they took their local styles of architecture with them. This weatherboarded cottage at Bells Yew Green would look quite at home in Massachusetts. Although the 'clapboard' houses of New England are sometimes painted green, grey, yellow and dark red, English weather-boarding, certainly in the Weald, is nearly always painted white.

ERIDGE GREEN, FRANT, SUSSEX

Extremely isolated and approached across fields and through deep steep beech woods, Forgewood Cottages were known to be the home of the manager of a forge in the 17th century. This part of Sussex used to be thick with forges when the oak forests provided fuel for smelting the iron. Cannon balls found in the little river that runs in front of the cottages suggest that armaments were being turned out here when the Cromwellian forces were holding Tunbridge Wells against the Royalists who held Southborough. In the 19th century coal mines took the iron and steel industry to other parts of the country, and in the 1890s the forgotten Forgewood Cottages were renovated, weatherboarded and probably inhabited by gamekeepers owing to their extreme remoteness.

SMARDEN, ASHFORD, KENT

Weatherboarding is an unpretentious material and was never seen on houses of the well-to-do, who would use tiles as a surface covering in preference. One of the important reasons for weatherboarding was to protect the timber frame of cottages. This became very necessary from the 18th century onwards when imported soft woods were used in place of good old English oak. In fact this cottage dates back to the 16th century when it was a farm, and was weatherboarded in the 18th century to protect its fabric. It was bought by Mr and Mrs Weeks over ninety years ago, and they brought up their eight children here. Two of their sons still live here.

Most of England's villages were natural evolutions, growing or diminishing over the centuries, but some were instant creations with instant communities which sprang up almost overnight on virgin land. It was the land-owning classes of the 18th century who first created these model villages; whether because they wished to improve the rural labourers' lot or wished to display magnanimity and wealth, or both, is irrelevant, for places such as Cambo in Northumberland, Sledmere in Yorkshire, Harlaxton in Lincolnshire, Hulcote in Northamptonshire, Compton Basset in Wiltshire, Lockinge in Berkshire, Albury in Surrey, Thorney in Huntingdonshire, and Hursley in Hampshire have survived the test of time by being well built and carefully maintained.

The face of England changed radically and rapidly in the 18th century, not least because a great step up in the number of enclosures caused criss-crossings of hedgerows and walls the length and breadth of the land. Land-owners enclosed and beautified their estates, and there was a burgeoning and then blossoming of landscaped parks, model villages and estate cottages. Admiral Russell, who lived at Chippenham in Cambridgeshire, was one of the first 'emparkers', and having demolished the old village next to his house to make way for a verdant park and artificial lake, he built a new model village of fifty one-storey semi-detached cottages between 1696 and 1704. The fashion for and convenience of model villages slowly gained momentum. James Bateman rebuilt the village of Well in Lincolnshire in 1730, John Emerton did the same at Thrumpton and Sir Thomas Perkins at Bradmoor, both in Nottinghamshire. By the 1760s 'Capability' Brown was busy sweeping away untidy villages to make way for rolling landscapes and lakes. In 1760 the first Earl of Harewood commissioned John Carr of York to build a village at Harewood in Yorkshire on Palladian lines, and in 1761 Lord Harcourt demolished the old village of Newnham Courtenay and built the new village of Nuneham Courtenay. The latter became a *cause célèbre* among the critics of model villages, both political and aesthetic, as did Milton Abbas in Dorset, the building of which from 1773 to 1786 by William Chambers in collaboration with 'Capability' Brown involved the destruction of a small market town.

Until the 19th century most model villages were built in relatively local styles on straight formal lines and it was not until 1810 that the first completely informal village

**LEVERTON,
HUNGERFORD,
BERKSHIRE**

This row of cottages built in brick with flint detailing and covered in a mustard-coloured wash was built in 1800 to house farm labourers on the Chilton Lodge Estate. John Pearce Esq., who owned Chilton Lodge at that time, must have realized that cottages of this calibre would add respectability to his estate when housing for the rural poor was in a terrible state all over England. 'The shattered hovels,' wrote the social observer Nathaniel Kent in the 1790s, 'which half the poor of this country are obliged to put up with, is truly affecting to a heart fraught with humanity.'

was built at Blaise Hamlet by John Nash in the then-novel Picturesque style. Its effect was revolutionary, for it was a complete reversal of ordered villages such as New Houghton in Norfolk. Many subsequent model villages followed Nash's blazing trail. The existing 17th-century village of Great Tew was redesigned on irregular lines by John Loudon who planted laurels and Irish yews to set off the ironstone of the cottage walls.

Examples of mid-19th-century model villages and especially estate cottages are legion and each estate usually has a consistent and distinctive style of architecture. Foreign travel was much easier by then and many architects had been influenced by Continental styles. Sir John Ingilby's village at Ripley, Yorkshire was re-vamped on Continental lines between 1830 and 1860; he even referred to his castle as his 'schloss' and had inscribed above his gatehouse 'Parlez au Suisse'. In 1838 Joseph Paxton's and John Robertson's collaboration at Edensor in Derbyshire incorporated Swiss chalet and Italian villa architecture, and Holly Village in Highgate, built by Darbishire in 1865, was more Bavarian than Ludwig. Architectural styles were not only chosen to swank of foreign travel but, more than at any other time, to display wealth, usually new. Samuel Morton Peto, a building and railway contractor, was typical of the new Victorian very rich and created a spectacular model village at Somerleyton in Suffolk in the late 1840s. Eminent architects were sometimes employed. In 1857 Sir Gilbert Scott was commissioned to build the village of Ilam in Staffordshire; between 1856 and 1858 William Butterfield built cottages and a church at Baldesbury St James in Yorkshire; Samuel Teulon built Hunstanworth in County Durham in 1863; Prince Albert built cottages at Sandringham in 1864; and at Aldford in Cheshire John Douglas designed one of the largest of all estate villages for the Duke of Westminster in 1866.

Model villages were not, however, confined to private estates. Industrialists, political independents and philanthropists followed the lead. As early as 1770 the master potter Josiah Wedgwood built a village for his workmen in Staffordshire and called it Etruria after an Etruscan vase. Non-conformists who had made strides in industry often felt especially responsible for their work forces; one such family were the Quaker Clarks who built cottages for their leather workers at Street in Somerset from 1829 onwards. In 1840 a complete model village was begun at Swindon in Wiltshire by Matthew Digby Wyatt to house workers on Brunel's Great Western Railway line, and in the 1850s Sir Titus Salt built 560 dwellings grouped spaciously around his enormous Italianate mill at Saltaire in Yorkshire. As the century wore on, some enlightened industrialists laid down ever brighter and healthier patterns for their villages, concentrating on gardens and facilities for outdoor recreation, of which the plans for Bournville near Birmingham provide a shining example. Built by the Cadburys for their chocolate factory workers with W. A. Harvey as architect, its planning was admired the world over, as was Mr Lever's village of Port Sunlight. The Crittalls heralded the Early Modern style with their village at Silver End in Essex which was begun in 1926 by the architect Sir Thomas Tait.

The Moravians were among the earliest of religious groups to build villages for themselves. A Chartist colony was begun in 1846 by Fergus O'Connor at Heronsgate; others followed at Lowbands, Snigs End, Minster Lovell and Great Dodford. Though each cottage was allotted one and a quarter acres, to encourage self-sufficiency, these land colonies failed, as did the colony at Whiteway founded by the Tolstoyan Anarchists in 1898. In the 1850s the Misses Talbot spent their considerable fortune on building a village to rehabilitate the poor families around Bournemouth and encourage high morals, and Lady Henry Somerset, who had faith in the 'fresh bracing air and scent of pine-woods as remedial agents', set up a village of Cottage Homes for Alcoholic Ladies at Duxhurst in Surrey in 1895.

Though industrialists kept their heads above water, the great agricultural slump of the 1880s hit land-owners and farmers so hard that by the 1900s the age of the grand model villages and cottages was on the decline. Only the phenomenally rich, like the Rothschilds and the Astors, could afford to house their farm labourers in any sort of lavish architectural style. Subdued schemes continued to be built, however, in a gentle way, and in a genteel Arts and Crafts style, notably at the village of Ardeley in Hertfordshire, designed in 1917 by F. C. Eden. But by this time the Government were becoming the major builders of both rural and urban housing. Raymond Erith's pair of farm labourers' cottages at Britwell Salome in Buckinghamshire built in 1971 is a good example of the tradition of distinctive estate architecture which is still just alive today.

NUNEHAM COURTENAY, OXFORD, OXFORDSHIRE

Following the fashion of the time Lord Harcourt decided in 1761 to sweep away the old village of Newnham Courtenay which was too close for comfort to his house, and rebuild a renamed Nuneham Courtenay. At first it was thought that Lord Harcourt had done a great service to his villagers by taking them from their 'hovels' and rehousing them in new, clean cottages. Tidiness was foremost – outhouses were tucked neatly away and an underground passage was provided for the cows so they were not seen passing from one pasture to another. However, the formal modernity of Nuneham Courtenay was not praised for long. The Picturesque movement was beginning to blossom and one of its innovators, William Gilpin, deplored Nuneham Courtenay as the antithesis of the Picturesque. Uvedale Price, a cult follower, said of the village, 'nothing can be more formal and insipid.'

LOWTHER, PENRITH, WESTMORLAND

Sir James Lowther commissioned the Adam brothers to design the model village of Lowther between 1765 and 1773. The original plan was extremely grandiose and the layout based on a Greek cross. In fact the scheme was only half completed, but nonetheless caused consternation. The cottages are of uniform pattern. A formal crescent broken in the centre forms the entrance to the village and a three-sided courtyard gives on to the village pump. There is a distinct feudal air about the place, with the bailiff's house standing like a sergeant major commanding the centre of the village. It must have amazed the traveller, set as it is in the wilds of Westmorland. In 1802 Richard Warner wrote in his *Tour Through Northern Counties*: 'stopped near new village of Lowther to stare at the fantastic incongruity of its plan which exhibits the grandest features of city architecture, the circus, the crescent and the square upon the mean scale of a peasant's cottage.'

BLAISE HAMLET, BRISTOL, SOMERSET

In 1810 the Quaker banker John Scandrett Harford commissioned John Nash to design the village of Blaise Hamlet in which to house his retired servants. Nash had certainly designed Picturesque cottages before, and even a two-floor dog kennel in the cottage style, but had never built a whole village. The unlevel site helped the irregular pattern of the village, and it is said that cottages faced in different directions, not for architectural reasons but to prevent neighbours from gossiping. Although he was to become the glittering architect of his age, building Brighton Pavilion and Regent's Park, Nash was often heard to say that no palace he ever planned gave him as much pleasure as that which he derived from his employment at Blaise Hamlet.

BLAISE HAMLET, BRISTOL, SOMERSET

Humphrey Repton, the famous landscape gardener, was also employed by John Harford to improve Blaise estate, but his relationship with John Nash was not a happy one and their informal partnership ended just before the building of Blaise Hamlet. Humphrey's son, George Repton, stayed with Nash until 1818, and was general supervisor while Nash was away journeying on other commissions. The village consists of nine wildly differing cottages scattered around a central green, whose focal point is the pump – Sweet Briar Cottage, Vine Cottage, Rose Cottage, Diamond Cottage, Jessamine Cottage, Oak Cottage, Dial Cottage, Circular Cottage and Double Cottage. Some are thatched, some tiled, and all sport elaborate chimneys of various shapes and sizes.

WHALLEY, CLITHEROE, LANCASHIRE

In 1829 John Taylor commissioned the architect George Webster of Kendal to build Moreton Hall, an enormous Neo-Jacobean mansion with 365 windows and 52 chimneys (demolished 1955). This row of cottages on the River Ribble was built around the same time to house estate workers. George Webster was particularly fond of the Gothic style and by 1830 had already built or enlarged three churches in Lancashire and Westmorland, whose ecclesiastical windows are unmistakably echoed here in Whalley. The Worsley family from Accrington came into Moreton Hall estate in the 1880s, adding Taylor to their name, and it is recorded that all the ground rents from the estate cottages were given to the governors of Whalley Grammar School.

WHALLEY, CLITHEROE, LANCASHIRE

Terrace Row is a familiar sight to users of the A59 road as it winds its way out of Whalley towards Billington. It was built to house estate workers by John Taylor of Moreton Hall in about 1830 and was almost certainly designed by George Webster. As the row backs into the steep rocky hillside, the ground floors were originally used as cellars, and elegant steps and a railed gallery lead to the next floor where accommodation consists of two rooms up and two rooms down. In 1924 Sir James Worsley-Taylor, who then owned the estate, sold Terrace Row to a local butcher, Mr Ralph Holgate, for £950. The latter then sold it to five separate private owners.

SCAMBLESBY TOP,
HORNCASTLE,
LINCOLNSHIRE

This grand Dutch façade of
whitewashed brick fronts an
ordinary cottage on the lonely
road from Horncastle to Louth.
Because of its isolation from the
rest of the country, Lincolnshire
was always a kingdom of its own
and its associations and influences
were more with the sea and with
Denmark and Holland than with
England. One third of it is even
referred to as Holland. What
Henry Thorold says in his
excellent Shell Guide to that
county is true – 'Lincolnshire is
the second largest county in
England and the least
appreciated.'

SELWORTHY, MINEHEAD,
SOMERSET

Thomas Dyke Acland, 10th
Baronet Holnicote, built the
village of Selworthy in 1828 as a
place of retirement for his estate
pensioners. Although he
employed no architect, he was
obviously directly influenced by
Nash's village of Blaise Hamlet,
and his copy of *Rural
Architecture* by P.F. Robinson
appears well thumbed and pencil-
marked. Sir Thomas took the
idea of the Picturesque to its
limits by insisting on the
inhabitants of Selworthy wearing
suitably romantic costumes and
encouraging them to congregate
under the walnut trees on the
village green. The visitor was
meant to be impressed by scenes
of pastoral bliss.

FRAMPTON UPON SEVERN,
STROUD,
GLOUCESTERSHIRE

The Gloucester and Sharpness
Canal was built to bypass the
shoals and shallows of the River
Severn and to restore
Gloucester's importance as an
inland port. It was completed in
1827, and the bridgemen's
cottages along it show the
transformation of canal
architecture from plain local
styles to highly fashionable ones.
No doubt the glorious spa town
of Cheltenham, not far away, and
largely built in the Grecian style
from 1800 to 1840, was a strong
influence on the canal company's
decision to give their model
cottages such distinction and
grandeur.

LOWSONFORD,
HENLEY-IN-ARDEN,
WARWICKSHIRE

Built about 1815, this lock
keeper's cottage with its strange
barrel-vaulted roof is a replica of
all the other cottages the length of
the Stratford-on-Avon Canal.
The canal company, being short
of money, were said to have left
the building of the cottages to the
navvies, and as they only knew
how to build tunnels, the cottages
came out tunnel-shaped. One of
the 19th-century bye-laws for the
'good government' of canals was
'. . . that if any Lock Keeper,
Wharfinger, or other Servant
belonging to the said Company of
Proprietors, shall give any
Preference, or shew Partiality to
any Boat, Barge, or other Vessel,
in passing through any Lock
upon the said intended Canal . . .
every Person so offending shall
forfeit and pay the Sum of
Twenty Shillings to the
Informer.'

EDENSOR, BAKEWELL, DERBYSHIRE

In 1835 the 6th Duke of Devonshire, together with his gardener Joseph Paxton, visited Nuneham Courtenay, which aroused no comment whatsoever in his diary, but a visit to Blaise Hamlet did: 'The most perfect cottages . . . I ever saw . . . Paxton was struck with the chimneys', he wrote. The Picturesque style was thus adopted on a grandiose scale in the building of the village of Edensor, which began in 1838, and boasted Norman, Swiss, Tudor and Gothic Revival cottages, set in spacious gardens. Paxton was in charge of the overall plan and his assistant John Robertson, who had been J. C. Loudon's draughtsman, saw to the details; but the Duke was certainly actively involved in the scheme. In 1839, on returning from a trip to Europe, he wrote in his diary, 'Fine day. Happy village. New cottages.' The church was built later in the 1860s by Gilbert Scott.

YELLOWHAM WOOD, DORCHESTER, DORSET

The Keeper's Cottage is described in Thomas Hardy's *Under The Greenwood Tree* as the home of Keeper Geoffrey Day, father of the heroine Fancy Day. The beamed ceiling in the front room and the leaded diamond glazing are described graphically. In reality, this cottage was the home of the Stinsford gamekeeper whose daughter Elizabeth (with whom Hardy was infatuated when he was about sixteen), is celebrated in Hardy's poem *Lizbie Browne*. One of the surviving trees in the grounds of this cottage is the Greenwood Tree of the title, beneath which the wedding dance took place.

OLD WARDEN,
BIGGLESWADE,
BEDFORDSHIRE

Between 1830 and 1850 existing
cottages at Old Warden were re-
vamped and new ones built in a
highly Picturesque style. Fancy
thatch and ornamental chimneys
echo Blaise Hamlet and suggest
that the architect, P.F.Robinson,
who was working nearby at the
time, had a strong hand in the
designing of Old Warden.

OLD WARDEN,
BIGGLESWADE,
BEDFORDSHIRE

Lord Ongley, under whose
auspices the village was built,
decided, as did the serious
followers of the Picturesque
movement, that inhabitants were
just as important as architecture
in pictorial terms. Thus he went
all the way and asked the
cottagers to wear tall hats and
voluminous red cloaks which
matched the paintwork on the
doors and windows.

HAWKESBURY UPTON,
TETBURY,
GLOUCESTERSHIRE

High on an escarpment
overlooking the Stroud Valley,
and commanding enormous
views, stands Monument
Cottage, built in 1846 to house
the custodian to this
extraordinary pagoda campanile.
The latter was built in memory of
General Lord Robert Somerset,
the fourth son of the 5th Duke of
Beaufort. The architect was
Lewis Vulliamy (son of the
celebrated clock maker), who
built Westonbirt, a gigantic
mansion nearby, in the Jacobean
style with one of the most famous
arboretums in the world.

GREAT TEW,
CHIPPING NORTON,
OXFORDSHIRE

The Old Tollgate Cottage, on a
road leading to the Great Tew
estate, has been little changed
since it was built around 1820. Its
present occupant of thirty years
still uses the well at the back and
has no mains water or electricity;
he also keeps pigs. In 1821
William Cobbett in his book
Cottage Economy wrote on
keeping pigs: '. . . much must
depend upon the situation of the
cottage . . . Even in lanes, or on
the sides of great roads, a pig will
find a good part of his food from
May to November; and, if he be
yoked, the occupiers of the
neighbourhood must be churlish
and brutish indeed if they give
the owner any annoyance.'

SWINDON, WILTSHIRE

Part of the Great Western Railway's model village, these cottages are built of Bath stone taken from the excavations of the Box Tunnel in 1840 when Brunel's railway was forging its way through the South-West. When the Marquess of Ailesbury refused to have such a monstrosity through Savernake Forest, Isambard Kingdom Brunel and the engineer Daniel W. Gooch decided on the small market town of Swindon as their centre of activities, and by 1853 nearly 250 cottages had been built to house the workers of the G.W.R.

SOUTHILL, BROOM, BEDFORDSHIRE

Having founded his brewery in London in 1742, the first Samuel Whitbread returned to his native Bedfordshire towards the end of his life and bought the Southill estate from the Byng family. His son took on the estate in 1796, and together with Henry Holland, the architect, set about improving his mansion, building new estate cottages and renovating old ones. This particular row of agricultural cottages was built around that time and then given a complete facelift in 1858 by a subsequent Mr Whitbread. Each cottage had a front garden which was to be kept neat at all times, and each was painted in the same livery of honey-coloured wash with dark green paintwork. The tradition continues today, and the direct descendants of the first Samuel Whitbread still live at Southill.

HOLLY VILLAGE, HIGHGATE, LONDON

In 1837, when she was only twenty-three, Baroness Burdett-Coutts inherited two million pounds from her banker grandfather. She paid little attention to inevitable male pursuit (although she developed an unrequited passion for the ageing Duke of Wellington) and instead devoted most of her time and money to alleviating the plight of the poor of London, either through housing or education. A well-known figure among eminent Victorians, she rocked society when, at the age of sixty, she married her American secretary who was half her age – a 'mad marriage', Queen Victoria called it. In 1865 she employed Henry Astley Darbishire to build Holly Village in which to house her retired servants, though it seems likely that many of the wilder and whackier embellishments were her idea rather than his. Seven single cottages and a double cottage round an arched gateway gave on to a central green set with monkey-puzzle trees; no fences or individual gardens were allowed, nor are they to this day, and so Holly Village remains a monument to that eccentric philanthropist.

HARKER, CARLISLE, CUMBERLAND

Part of a scattered group of Victorian estate cottages built in chequered brick, which was a very characteristic feature in this area. Crusts of impurities found in the local clay of western Cumberland, instead of being discarded, were made into bricks which when fired varied in colour from white to grey, and were used to relieve the monotony of red bricks on houses and cottages in the district. Once a picture of rurality, this cottage now stands a hundred yards from the M6 motorway, and is the only one of five to have survived in its original state without the addition of pebble-dash and plate-glass windows.

LETHERINGSETT, ERPINGHAM, NORFOLK

In the well-wooded valley of the Glaven stands a row of three estate cottages built in 1871 by the Cozens-Hardy family. They are a fine example of the use of dressed flint together with bricks produced fifty yards away in the field behind. The last Lord Cozens-Hardy died in 1975 and it was one of his predecessors, William Hardy, who 'clothed these once barren hills with foliage' as recorded on his epitaph in the churchyard. Even Cobbett was impressed by Hardy's work in laying out and improving the estate, and subsequent Cozens-Hardys kept up the good work.

ASHBY DE LA LAUNDE, SLEAFORD, LINCOLNSHIRE

In John Wood of Bath's pattern book devoted entirely to cottages, *Series Of Plans For Cottages Or Habitations Of The Labourer*, published in 1781, semi-detached dwellings are favoured so that neighbours could easily be of assistance to each other in times of need, particularly in remote rural areas. This plan was also cheaper to build and was a common pattern for estate cottages throughout the 19th century. However, Wood's innocent supposition that all next-door neighbours would automatically be friends cannot always have been the case; the left-hand of this cottage is called The Fort, the right Stonelea – even the door is divided in colour – denoting remarkable independence on both sides.

GLANDFORD-CUM-
BAYFIELD, HOLT,
NORFOLK

This cottage is part of the model
village built by Sir Alfred Jodrell
of Bayfield Hall at the end of the
19th century. It houses the
custodian of the shell museum
which was built at the centre of
the village to display the
thousands of shells collected by
Sir Alfred and his two sisters.
The cottage has dutch gables in
keeping with the rest of the
village and is built of flint dug
from the nearby pit at Bayfield
Brecks. Sir Alfred also rebuilt the
church at Glandford, on a lavish
scale, in memory of his mother.

ERIDGE GREEN, FRANT,
SUSSEX

Originally built as a school by the
Abergavenny family in the much
favoured Tudor-Revival style of
the period (1880s), Staircase
Cottage is now a private dwelling.
Even by the end of the 19th
century children were still
inextricably involved in the
financial survival of their parents
and would often work instead of
going to school if called upon.
The summer holidays in this area
were called 'hopping holidays',
and an October 1873 entry in the
school log book of a nearby
village reads: 'Opened school
today after the hopping holiday.
Attendance rather small, children
not quite ready to come. Some
are waiting to buy shoes.'
Another entry of 1880 reads:
'Attempted to open school but
found it impossible to do so for
the girls were out gleaning and
hop picking.'

PORT SUNLIGHT, BIRKENHEAD, CHESHIRE

The concept of the estate village as a model community for estate workers was followed by some large manufacturers for their factory workers. William Hesketh Lever started his empire by expanding his family grocery business, and by 1887 Sunlight Soap was the best selling brand on the market. Although the unions were against his Utopian housing scheme and decried it as an attempt to exonerate capitalism, Lever's heart was nonetheless with Port Sunlight from the cutting of the first sod by Mrs Lever in 1888 until his death in 1925. Lever even lived in the village himself and when addressing the crowd at the opening ceremony sincerely hoped that his workers would learn from living in pleasant surroundings 'that there is more enjoyment in life than the mere going to and returning from work and looking forward to Saturday night to draw wages.'

PORT SUNLIGHT, BIRKENHEAD, CHESHIRE

William Owen, the Company architect, drew up the first plan for twenty-eight cottages. Gradually many architects were involved, notably John Douglas and William & Segar. Anne Hathaway's cottage was faithfully reproduced, Kenyon Hall reappeared as a cottage group, and every sort of architectural style was used. Together with Mr Cadbury's village of Bournville, Port Sunlight broke down the distinctions between housing for workers and housing for others, and became a model for town planners. The musical *The Sunshine Girl*, produced in 1912, took Port Sunlight for its setting, and Harold Wilson met his future wife at the tennis club here. There is still a waiting list to obtain a cottage in Port Sunlight today.

HEVER, EDENBRIDGE, KENT

In 1903 Mr William Waldorf Astor made a successful bid for Hever Castle. Dazzling though its beauty and historical associations were (it was the home of Anne Boleyn), Hever had one drawback for Mr Astor – it was not large enough. Rather than extend this small and perfect moated castle, a village of random cottages in the Tudor style was planned beside it, to house his myriad guests and staff. Mr F.L.Pearson was employed as architect and by 1904 there were 748 workmen engaged upon the village, Castle and pleasure grounds. (This was before the work of excavating the nearby lake began which occupied another 800 men.) In order to make room for the proposed village it was necessary to push back a river bed some hundred yards to the north of its natural course, and a glazed tiled basement was built in a series of arches twenty feet below the ground. The walls of the cottages taken in cross-section are composed of plaster, lath, copper sheeting, asphalt, asbestos, chicken wire, more lath and finally plaster outside. Although from the outside the village looks like a haphazard collection of forty or fifty Tudor cottages, each cottage is in fact connected to the next by corridors and the whole is connected to the Castle by a covered bridge.

BUDLEIGH SALTERTON, DEVONSHIRE

Lawrence Weaver, when writing on the economies of rural building in the early 1900s when these farm labourers' cottages were built at South Farm, proffered the following advice: 'A rectangular plan is most convenient and cheapest. By building more than one cottage in a block the following savings can be made. On a pair £7 10s to £12 10s per cottage; on three £10 to £17 each. In bedrooms space must always be provided for double beds; cottagers do not use single beds. The provision of a bath is debatable because it is apt to be used for any other purpose than bathing.'

In the 18th century, the upper crust were eager to display to one another, and to the rest of the world, that they were both cultivated and literate. They had ample money to beautify their parks and ample time on their hands to visit other people's. The building of Picturesque cottages became one of their favourite aesthetic indulgences, and was undertaken in a style which had its roots firmly planted in nature and Gothic ruins and its mossy branches inextricably interwoven with the romantic paintings of Claude and Poussin and pastoral poems of William Shenston and James Thomson. It was a conscious effort to try and incorporate the beauty of landscape, the romance of ruins, the natural disorder of cottage architecture, the sublime and the beautiful, into a building which would inspire in the spectator nostalgia and romantic sentiment. Picturesque cottages were to be viewed from the comfort of a carriage while touring an estate, or glimpsed across landscaped parks through drawing-room windows – a symbol of idyllic pastoralism as well as a sign that their creators were men of culture and sensibility.

By the middle of the 18th century, architects like William Kent were already relating buildings to landscape and Thomas Wright was busy creating rustic fantasies of curved tree trunks and fossils. Batty Langley, in his *Gothic Architecture Restored & Improved* (1742), was advocating a return to the Gothic of the 13th and 14th centuries as displayed in many a ruined abbey; Horace Walpole began remodelling his home at Strawberry Hill, Twickenham, in the Gothic Revival style as did Sir Roger Newdigate at Arbury Hall, Warwickshire, and estate owners were beginning to build thatched and rustic follies in their parks from Stourhead to Stowe. But it was not until the 1780s that the word 'Picturesque' was formally introduced by one of its staunchest supporters, William Gilpin. Gilpin was a schoolmaster and the Vicar of Boldre in Hampshire who spent his holidays sketching romantic countryside all over Britain, but perhaps most famously in Cumberland and Westmorland whose rugged natural scenery inspired his senses to an extreme degree. 'The rules of picturesque beauty', he said, 'are drawn from nature . . . all the formalities of hedge-row trees, and square divisions of property, are disgusting to a high degree'. He was happy to improve nature if necessary by clothing mountains with 'the drapery of a little wood' and suggested that cattle grazing in the ideal landscape should be any other colour than black and white 'which make together the most

DOYDEN, PORTQUIN, CORNWALL

Built in 1830 by Samuel Symons Esq., this one-up-one-down cottage in the Gothic Picturesque style was erected solely for the purpose of drinking and gambling. It might also have served as an eye-catcher from the ancient manor farm of Roscarrock – an early example of landscaping using the sea to appear as a series of lakes between the headlands.

121

inharmonious of all mixtures'. Actual people walking about in Gilpin's dream-like scenes were treated as Picturesque appendages and should, he said, be clad preferably in 'long, folding draperies such as soldiers, gypsies or banditti'. The theories of Gilpin's return to pastoralism had a profound effect on his contemporaries and the appearance of articles in *The Gentleman's Magazine* did much to influence the national viewpoint, comparing the 'superior elegance, richness and grace' of ruins and Gothic architecture to the 'ridiculous and contemptible plainness and simplicity of the Grecian'.

Together with an unprecedented amount of sentimental theory from Sir Uvedale Price, Richard Payne Knight and others came an unprecedented amount of elaborate designs for Picturesque cottages in the pattern books of the day. David Laing's *Hints for Dwellings* (1801), Pocock's *Architectural Designs for Rustic Cottages and Picturesque Dwellings* (1807), Papworth's *Designs for Rural Residences* (1818), and P. F. Robinson's *Rural Architecture, or a series of designs for ornamental Cottages* (1823) were amongst the most well known. Picturesque eye-catchers popped up in people's parks as gamekeepers' cottages, dairies, menageries and dog-kennels, as an indication of cultivated taste. Thatch, a compulsory appendage to the rustic look, dripped copiously over bold overhanging eaves. Pointed windows were set in irregular shaped walls of unequal height, all hopefully blending and harmonizing with the landscape. Instead of sweeping away untidy cottages as 'Capability' Brown had done, Humphrey Repton homed in on the lonely cottage in the park, dressed it with leaded lights and scalloped barge-boards, and topped it with an exaggerated chimney for, he said, 'there is hardly anything more picturesque and pleasing than smoke curling amongst trees'.

Cottages in parks became mere garden furniture or theatrical sets, and far more attention was given to filling in pediments with attractively arranged twigs or attaching split logs to walls in pleasing patterns than was paid to the actual accommodation behind the façade. This usually consisted of a sitting-room and at the most two bedrooms with a porch in front where preferably its rustic inhabitants would linger, suitably clothed in flowing robes, while the land-owner and his guests were touring the estate. (It was not until Blaise Hamlet was built by Nash in 1810 that rural inhabitants were as comfortable as the style of their cottages was Picturesque.) J. C. Loudon gave instructions, perhaps about Great Tew, which he prettified in the Picturesque style around 1811, that there should 'always be children playing and villagers passing to and fro to contribute to the rural effect of the scene'. Ivy, roses, creepers and moss were encouraged, as were pastoral scenes – and instead of fences, children of 'poor but worthy cottagers prettily disguised as shepherds might be employed to keep the sheep from straying'. In the village of Selworthy in Somerset, villagers were encouraged to linger on the green, and in Old Warden, Bedfordshire, they were asked to wear red cloaks and bonnets to match the paintwork of the cottages.

Picturesque cottages were not only built for the rustic inhabitant to be gazed upon romantically by the rich, however; in larger and more comfortable forms they even became the homes and holiday and sporting retreats of the latter. Generally called *cottages ornés*, they were advertised in pattern books with liberal lacings of poetry. The Duke of Bedford's Endsleigh Cottage and George IV's fanciful Royal Lodge in Windsor Great Park set fashionable examples. *Cottages ornés* were built at a rate of knots in Richmond and Roehampton, Brighton and Sidmouth. The emergent middle classes, rich tradesmen and industrialists decided that to own a thatched cottage in the country was no longer a social disgrace, so long as it was sufficiently ornate and commodious. The search for romance, despite the Napoleonic Wars and their aftermath, increased, and more and more elaborately fretworked barge-boards burgeoned on 'cottages' in the unlikeliest of places from the Arcadian slopes of the Lune Valley in Lancashire to the ordinary outskirts of Oswestry in Shropshire.

As the cult became all the rage the term 'Picturesque' blurred at its rustic and Gothic Revival edges with a profusion of added styles from Italian to Russian and the word 'cottage' to describe a large dwelling got completely out of hand. By the 1840s the original concept, born among the mossy stones and hills of the Lake District in the 18th century, had been lost among theatrical exaggerations. Variations of the original theme were being taken up by all and sundry, even the railway companies. For the élite, the vogue for the true Picturesque was over. Seduced instead by the Italian Lakes and the warm coast of the South of France, they began to sell or let their *cottages ornés* by the English sea, and their rustic dreams quietly crumbled in forgotten corners of the park.

BADMINTON, SODBURY, GLOUCESTERSHIRE

The thatched umbrella cottage in the village of Badminton, also by Thomas Wright, was one of the earliest *cottages ornés* in England and pre-dates Blaise Hamlet by sixty years. Until recently Wright was best known as an astronomer and philosopher; but from the 1740s he designed many arbours, grottoes and summer-houses in rustic, Gothic, Palladian and castellated styles at such power houses as Nuthall, Nottinghamshire, and Shugborough, Staffordshire. In 1746 the 4th Duke of Beaufort employed William Kent to tart up his park and garden, but the latter died two years later and so the embellishments were left entirely up to 'The Wizard'. He went to town in no uncertain manner and provided the Park with, among other things, a wildly rustic thatched Root House, and a farm which, from a distance, looked like a large fortified village in France.

BADMINTON, SODBURY,
GLOUCESTERSHIRE

Looking much like a toy castle,
this castellated cottage was
designed by Thomas Wright,
'The Wizard of Durham', for the
4th Duke of Beaufort in about
1750. Wright was born near
Bishop Auckland, the son of a
yeoman carpenter. Because of a
speech impediment he left school
early and studied privately with a
local mathematician and
astronomer. By the age of
fourteen he confessed to being
'much in love with
Mathematicks, and very much
given to the Amusements of
Drawing, Planning of Maps and
Buildings.' By the age of twenty-
five he had been taken up by the
Earl of Pembroke, who paid for
his model of a hemispherian, and
introduced him to the King.
Before long he was orbiting in
high society and would often
oblige with designs for gardens
and garden buildings.

STOURHEAD, MERE, WILTSHIRE

This thatched cottage built of rocky stone and known as The Convent in the Woods was designed to be visited by carriage from the main house over a mile away. It was built between 1760 and 1770 by the great Henry Hoare II of the banking family, who was responsible for the creation of the now world-famous Stourhead Gardens and Park. Turrets, obelisks, Gothic windows and a belfry combined to give the cottage a suitably ecclesiastical air and to kindle philosophical thoughts in the hearts of onlookers. Originally it had painted panels inside displaying nuns in the dress of different orders, and contained glass from Glastonbury.

LOWER SWELL, STOW-ON-THE-WOLD, GLOUCESTERSHIRE

India in the Cotswolds. A carbonated chalybeate spring was discovered here in 1807 and this small spa was built, now known as Spa Cottages. It seems certain that Samuel Pepys Cockerell designed the central façade of Spa Cottages at about the same time as he was commissioned by his brother Sir Charles Cockerell to build nearby Sezincote, the forerunner to the Brighton Pavilion. The fir-cone and honeysuckle finials, the pineapple over the door, and the altogether Eastern appearance was far too daring a style for a local builder to copy so soon after Sezincote. Cockerell used considerable originality in his architectural designs, notably in the steeple which he designed for St Anne's Church, Soho.

127

SIDMOUTH, DEVONSHIRE

Probably the most picturesque
council house in England,
Pauntley Cottage was presented
to the town of Sidmouth by
Viscount Hambledon early this
century. It was built in about
1810 at a time when Bath was
becoming less fashionable and
Sidmouth increasingly popular as
a watering place. Though never
quite as gay or raucous as
Brighton, Sidmouth attracted
royalty and nobility and many a
mistress was set up here, all
enjoying the new fad of
'rusticating' by the seaside.

LYME REGIS, DORSET

W. F. Pocock, in his book
*Architectural Designs for Rustic
Cottages, Picturesque Dwellings,
Villas, Etc.*, which came out in
1807, referred to cottages such as
this one at Lyme Regis as
'cabanes ornées'. He suggested
that cottages such as these
'should afford the necessary
conveniences for persons of
refined manners and habits'.
Built in the early 19th century on
a hill road leading out of the
town, this unique *cottage orné* was
originally a toll house. Polygonal
in plan, its domed thatched roof
is trimmed at the eaves to create
an umbrella effect, and its deep
overhang is supported on wooden
angle posts.

ENDSLEIGH,
MILTON ABBOT,
DEVONSHIRE

A ducal idea of a cottage. The 6th
Duke of Bedford's wife,
Georgina, was in love with the
Romantic Revival style and was
behind the building of Endsleigh
Cottage, designed by Sir Jeffry
Wyatville, and begun in 1810. Sir
Humphrey Repton was engaged
to create a landscape to enhance
the setting of this elaborate
cottage orné, and by 1818
Endsleigh estate was described as
'The Garden Paradise of the
West'. For over a century the
Dukes of Bedford, accompanied
by an army of retainers,
descended on Endsleigh Cottage
for a few weeks every year to fish
and hunt. It was sold in 1953 and
is now a summer guest house.

SIDMOUTH, DEVONSHIRE

Clifton Cottage, The Beacon and
Rock Cottage were built at the
end of the 18th century when
Sidmouth was becoming a
popular resort with the nobility,
the fashionable and the genteel
who ventured towards the sea and
even stepped into it. George IV's
physicians prescribed the
following directions for bathing,
which had recently become so
popular: 'The most proper time
for bathing is early in the
morning before which no exercise
should be taken; all previous
fatigues tending to diminish that
force which the fibres when
contracted will otherwise have of
removing obstructions more
effectually; one of the great ends
sought for bathing ... To bathe
late in the day will occasion great
depression of the spirits.'

BUDLEIGH SALTERTON,
DEVONSHIRE

Fairlynch is a marine *cottage orné*
built by a local ship owner in
1811 with a thatched lookout
tower, chapel windows and
containing a double wing
staircase inside. No doubt he was
inspired by the already numerous
flights of fancy which were being
built in ever increasing romantic
styles from the end of the 18th
century onwards.

SIDMOUTH, DEVONSHIRE

Old Cotmaton Cottage was built
in 1830. Horace Walpole's
Thames-side villa, Strawberry
Hill, at Twickenham had set a
fashionable pattern for rural
retreats in the Gothic style and
suggested romance to retired
Colonial administrators and
military men who liked
verandahs, spacious lawns and
the sometimes sunny climes of
Devon.

AMBLESIDE, WESTMORLAND

Local legend has it that the cottage on the bridge over the Stock Ghyll in the middle of Ambleside was built by a Scotsman who wished to avoid land tax. However it was almost certainly built as a folly or summer-house in the 18th century for Old Ambleside Hall. In 1840 it became the home of a Mr Rigg, who brought up six children in it. This must certainly have meant that the whole family slept in the same bed. A writer for the *Saturday Review* in 1858 said that cramped cottage life was bound to lead to a life of harlotry, 'great boys and girls, mothers and fathers, all sleeping in one room led to boldness and shamefulness. The cottage bedroom was the first stop to the Haymarket'.

MARLBOROUGH,
WILTSHIRE

Originally inhabited by a
Carmelite order from 1316 to
1538, The Priory in Marlborough
High Street was demolished in
1820 by the Merriman family
who built a new house on its site
using bits of the old stonework.
In the mid-19th century a
Captain Price bought the
property and, wishing to
aggrandize it, made a fashionably
meandering drive bridging the
River Kennet and punctuated it
with this lodge cottage, a
miniature castle of flint and brick
with a pebble-dash extension,
which also incorporates
fragments of the original Priory.

135

FINCHINGFIELD, ESSEX

As early as the 1750s the
Halfpenny brothers, in their
pattern book *The Country
Gentleman's Pocket Companion*,
were advocating pentagonal
lodges in the 'Gothic taste' and
said they could be built 'in a good
Manner for the sum of eighty
four pounds.' Like Batty
Langley, the Halfpenny brothers
were ahead of their time and this
pentagonal lodge, almost an exact
replica of their design, was not
built until around 1800 when the
'Gothic taste' was beginning to be
accepted and safe. It was built by
the Ruggles family of Spains Hall
(Sir Evelyn Ruggles-Brises,
1857–1935, founded Borstal).

SHRIVENHAM, BERKSHIRE

In the 1850s Lord Barrington and
his new wife returned from a
blissful honeymoon in
Switzerland and determined to
build a replica of the chalet in
which they had stayed. Swiss
Cottage was the result and
became a playhouse for their
subsequent children. The Swiss
Chalet at Osborne in the Isle of
Wight, built for Queen Victoria's
children at about the same time,
may easily have influenced them.
The estate on which it stands has
long since been lost under main
roads and the gradual spread of
Shrivenham.

**ENDSLEIGH,
MILTON ABBOT,
DEVONSHIRE**

As part of Sir Humphrey Repton's landscaping, the Swiss Cottage at Endsleigh was built in about 1812 to be seen from the main cottage, to the designs of Sir Jeffry Wyatville. The ground and top floors were occupied by an estate worker and on the middle floor the Duchess of Bedford stored her china collection. There was a separate privy outside which was kept for the use of the Duke and his guests when out hunting. The cottage was later used for afternoon cream teas. The cladding is of split oak logs and the verandah has oak beams and posts. The cottage has recently been saved from dereliction by the Landmark Trust, who bought it in 1977 and have restored it to its full glory.

**BARHAM, IPSWICH,
SUFFOLK**

The fad for the Picturesque and the imitation of the primitive rural cottage did not confine itself to English rurality; Scottish Baronial, Italian, Russian and Swiss cottage styles became inordinately popular. This Swiss cottage, in the grounds of Shrubland Hall, was probably built by a local architect in the 1860s for Admiral Sir George Brook Middleton, who fought in the Crimean War.

CHILTON FOLIAT,
RAMSBURY, WILTSHIRE

Riverside Cottage, on the banks
of the River Kennet, was built in
the early half of the last century
as a fishing cottage for the nearby
Littlecote Estate. Decidedly
Picturesque with its leaded
panes, stags' horns and rustic
porch with a built-in seat, it
served to house fishing rods and
tackle and would have been the
scene of many Victorian picnics.
More recently it has been the
home of the Water Bailiff.

IXWORTH, THINGOE,
SUFFOLK

An early Victorian eye-catcher
which echoes the rustic church
of Ixworth Thorpe with its
thatched roof. Despite the
inconvenience of arranging
furniture inside, polygonal
cottages were by now widely
advocated in pattern books, and
became a popular style with the
gentry who thought that building
Picturesque cottages on their
estates showed an educated eye
and a refined taste. In his famous
essay on *The Sublime and
Beautiful*, written at the end of
the 18th century, Edmund Burke
suggested that 'a true artist
should put a generous deceit on
the spectators, and effect the
noblest designs by easy methods.'
It looks as if this advice was taken
a bit too literally in the case of
this cottage, which appears to
have no real windows at all, but
only pretend ones.

CHATSWORTH, BAKEWELL, DERBYSHIRE

In 1825 the famous 'Bachelor' Duke of Devonshire went to Moscow to attend the coronation of Tsar Nicholas I, as George IV's representative. He made a firm friend of the Tsar and came back to Chatsworth laden with gifts and mementoes – clocks, sleighs and malachite. He also brought a Russian coachman with him who stayed with the family for many years. Soon after his return, inspired by the glories of Russia, he built this cottage high up in the wood above Chatsworth, to house a keeper and his family, which it has done ever since. The barge-boards and shutters could possibly have been brought from Russia in the Bachelor Duke's luggage and a former keeper remembers them being brightly painted *à la Russe* up until the beginning of this century.

BARHAM, IPSWICH, SUFFOLK

In the 1840s, when the dinner hour had been advanced to half past seven or eight o'clock, and the gap between lunch and dinner became inordinately long, ladies with healthy appetites began to have tea and cakes, at first surreptitiously in their bedrooms and then more openly in their drawing rooms and summer houses. The Duchess of Rutland was officially serving tea by 1850, and so it became an accepted routine. Guests, while appraising the gardens, especially those stupendously laid out by Charles Barry at Shrubland Hall for the Middleton family, might stop to take tea in this Russian Lodge, dispensed by the hostess from an elegant samovar.

CHERINGTON, TETBURY,
GLOUCESTERSHIRE

This school-mistress's cottage is
in the beautiful and
unadulterated stone village of
Cherington which is situated at
the head of a valley with a lake
beneath it. The cottage was built
in 1850 at the same time as the
school to which it is attached.
The view, with a ha-ha before it,
gives on to wide corn fields. The
school was closed down in the
1970s.

BOWOOD, CALNE,
WILTSHIRE

When the 2nd Earl of Shelburne
employed 'Capability' Brown to
remodel his park at Bowood in
the 1760s, part of the scheme
involved flooding a valley to form
a lake. A village at the bottom of
the valley was swept away, and its
occupants were re-housed in the
new model village of Sandy Lane
about a mile away. However, the
right of way through the lost
village had to be maintained and
so this ferry cottage was built to
provide a 24-hour service across
the lake. The lattice windows, tall
chimney and verandah were
romantic 19th-century
embellishments to create a
pleasant eye-catcher for Bowood
House.

HODNET,
MARKET DRAYTON,
SHROPSHIRE

Paradise Lodge was built by the
Heber Percy family in the 1870s
to complement the style of their
new home, Hodnet Hall. 'The
entrance lodge to a country park
may be considered as a superior
kind of cottage' wrote C. J.
Richardson in *The Englishman's
House* (1870). 'It is often
occupied by some favourite
domestic or other attaché of the
family. It is usually placed in a
prominent position, dressed with
surrounding trees, and with
accompanying gates, posts, and
rails. Considerable attention is
always paid to the lodge. An ugly
one is an exception, and is very
seldom seen.' Bishop Heber, the
early Victorian hymn writer who
wrote *From Greenland's Icy
Mountains*, lived at Hodnet Hall
and was Rector of Hodnet.

ONIBURY, CRAVEN ARMS,
SHROPSHIRE

The Railway companies of the
19th century were intent on
creating every aspect of railways
as being full of adventure and
wonder. This they certainly were,
and Victorian track-side
architecture evoked all the
romance and excitement of this
revolutionary mode of travel.
Owned by the Shropshire Union
Canal & Railway Company, and
later sold to the Great Western
Railway Company, Onibury
Station opened in 1865 and was
closed by Dr Beeching in 1957.
The present private owner still
has the last ticket issued at the
station and has made his home in
the station master's cottage and
the former waiting room. It is
painted in the blue and white
colours of the Caledonian
Railway Company.

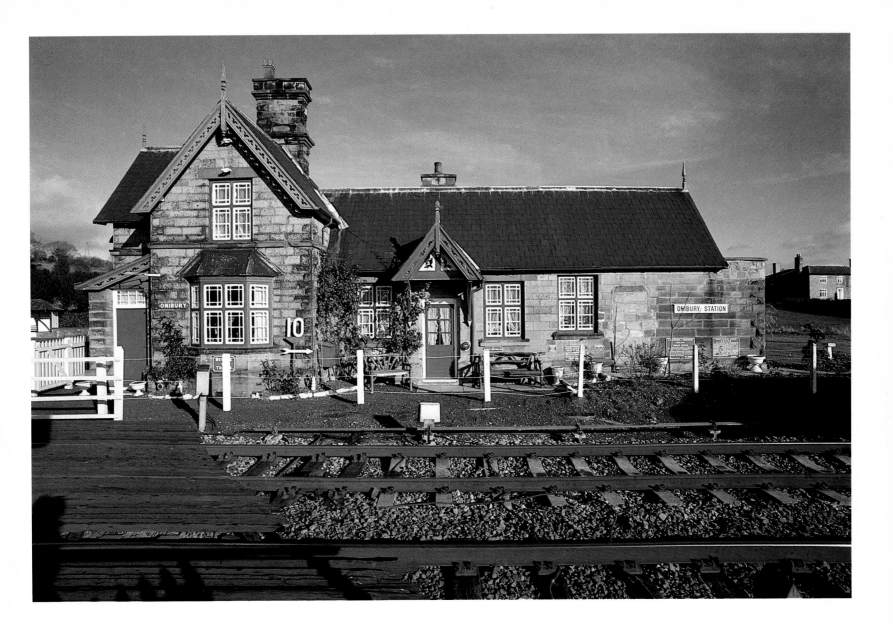

147

SIDMOUTH, DEVONSHIRE

By the 1850s the fashion for Sidmouth was declining in the eyes of high society who ventured instead to Nice and Monte Carlo; but nevertheless it remained a popular resort with the middle classes. There is no doubt that Romantic Victorian cottages such as Balfour Lodge stemmed from the *cottages ornés* of the late Georgians and from Nash's and Wyatville's flights of originality; but by this time the term 'Picturesque' had lost its pastoral image.

SIDMOUTH, DEVONSHIRE

Sidmouth provided a gentle alternative to those who were denied Continental travel by the Napoleonic Wars. After the publication of such books as Lugar's *Sketches of Cottage Architecture* (1807), substantial dwellings – often far from cottages as they were fashionably called – were built with prospects of the sea by elegant society folk. Instead of building from scratch, Lord Gwydir bought this manor house in 1817, extended and re-vamped it in the Gothic style, and renamed it Woodlands Cottage. In 1856 it was bought by Mr Johnstone, who replaced the thatch with hexagonal slates cut at enormous cost, and embellished the gables with stone sugar-icing bargeboards, prepared in Italy, shipped to England, and brought to Woodlands Cottage by horse and cart.

The true traditions of cottage architecture, lost in the uniformity of back-to-back artisans' dwellings which were spreading like strawberry jam over England, came back with a wondrous home-made bang with the Arts and Crafts architects of the late 19th century. 'The velvet of thatch, the soft warm tile, the hoary roughness of stone', as Edward Prior described them in 1889, saw the new bright light of the Edwardian summer. The secret of Arts and Crafts architecture lay not in its imitation of past styles but in its ingenious and original adaptation of those styles to create solid, practical and comfortable homes. It took the best traditional features, and made them work as they had never worked before. Outside chimney stacks, soaring up roughcast walls, actually made the fires draw and the pine logs blaze in the inglenook; sitting-room windows faced south and west and saw more sun than ever before; doors of seasoned wood with practical hinges and latches opened and shut with quiet ease in many a gentle homestead up and down the land. The touch and feel of things was as important as the look of them – everything was hand-made and often the architect would design not only the building but all that went in it from the furniture and fabrics to the window catches and cutlery.

The ancestors of the Arts and Crafts movement were the great Victorian architects like Butterfield, Scott, Burges, Street, the Gothic Revival prophet Pugin and the theorist and critic Ruskin. Its contemporary leaders included Norman Shaw, whose use of local materials and building traditions and whose innovatory garden suburb at Bedford Park in Middlesex in 1878, among other things, made him the giant of his day. Edward Godwin, too, had a strong influence on the movement; lover of Ellen Terry, friend of Oscar Wilde, he shocked, rocked and rippled the Arts and Crafts tide with his search for modernity in architecture. But perhaps the most famous innovators of all were William Morris and Philip Webb. Morris studied divinity at Oxford, architecture under Street, and painting under Rosetti; he commissioned Philip Webb to build his home and started a firm to furnish its every nook and cranny (later Morris & Co.); he lectured on the need to abolish the ugliness of towns, advocating a return to mediaevalism, and was a founder of socialism. His influence on younger architects was gigantic. In 1884 William Lethaby and Edward Prior along with others founded the Art Workers' Guild in Bloomsbury, which soon became the working and social club, the home-from-home for many Arts and

ULVERSCROFT,
LEICESTER,
LEICESTERSHIRE

Stoneywell, one of the finest examples of Arts and Crafts cottage architecture, was built by Ernest Gimson in 1898–9 in the strange rolling countryside of Charnwood Forest, near Leicester. Originally thatched, it is anchored to the ground by a massive chimney, and its Z shape zig-zags down the rocky hillside, blending with the surrounding landscape. Ernest Gimson was a strong influence in the Arts and Crafts movement and was helped in the building of Stoneywell Cottage by his assistant, Detmar Blow.

ASHBY ST LEDGERS,
DAVENTRY,
NORTHAMPTONSHIRE

Edwin Lutyens was the eleventh
child of a soldier turned painter,
and had little education except
for the year he spent in the office
of the architect Sir Ernest
George. Lutyens began building
in Surrey and by 1906, when he
built this row of cottages for the
Hon. Ivor Guest, later Lord
Ashby St Ledgers, he was among
the top Arts and Crafts architects
of his day (he went on to become
the most famous Grand Manner
architect and was later knighted).
When they were built, each
cottage boasted a kitchen,
scullery, parlour and three
bedrooms. A porch at the back
served as a covered way to the
fuel house and earth closet. Old
masonry was used for the lower
walls and the upper parts were of
brick roughcast.

Crafts architects. Sedding, Pite, Ricardo, Voysey, Gimson, Lutyens, Blow, Shaw, Ashbee, Mackmurdo and many others visited it and exchanged views on all aspects of art and craft. Some shared Morris's left-wing ideals; some, like the high church Norman Shaw and the doctrinaire Voysey, did not; but whatever their religious or political differences were they were all exceptional architects. From Voysey's simple lines to Gimson's organic shapes, from Lutyens's independence to Baillie Scott's romance, there was a blend of the best traditional styles with complete originality.

With this new wave of Arts and Crafts architecture came a new wave of Arts and Crafts homesteaders; and suburban railways, electric tramcars, cheap land and especially the cheap sandy soil of Surrey helped them on their way. Romantic business men, consciously progressive families, and early socialists trickled into the country, not to hunt and shoot through it, but to walk through it; not to return to marble halls and roast pheasant for dinner but to return to textured walls and lentil soup eaten with hand-wrought spoons by Baillie Scott, sitting on ladder-back chairs by Voysey. Their submission to nature in the architecture of their homes materialized as well in their gardens – in wild informal borders, crazy paving and drifts of daffodils. Following Gertrude Jekyll's boot prints, women in sandals wrote books about their Surrey gardens and were apt to live on nuts and salad, having spent their meat money on herbaceous plants.

Morris's mediaeval revival dream of simplicity had a profound effect which is still echoed now, though not the universal effect he had hoped for – 'art for the people by the people'. The flaw in the homespun fabric of Arts and Crafts architecture lay in the fact that craftsmen cost more than machines and the homes conceived for the masses to combat the uniform ugliness of industrial housing became the homes of men with more than moderate means, with the few exceptions of specially commissioned cottages for labourers such as Clough Williams-Ellis's cottages at Cornwell in Oxfordshire, Lutyens's Ashby St Ledgers and Detmar Blow's cottages at Wilsford.

The Arts and Crafts movement saw the best and last of traditional cottage architecture. Attempts to revive it died slow deaths down dreary lengths of ribbon development as the economic merits of mass production knocked it on the head for good.

WILSFORD, AMESBURY, WILTSHIRE

Detmar Blow, who built this dairyman's cottage in 1905, was a dedicated follower of the Arts and Crafts movement, and was greatly influenced by Ruskin, Lethaby, Prior and Gimson. He was very good indeed at getting his buildings to look genuine, sometimes more genuine than the real thing. George Morris and Esther Wood, writing in 1906, put it in a nutshell: 'The building should never give the impression of a ready-made thing taken out of a workshop and suddenly set down upon the site. Rather it should hug the ground as if it loved it, as if it were born of the very spirit of the place. A few of our modern architects have admirably fulfilled these conditions . . . Such men as Mr Philip Webb and Mr E.E. Lutyens in Surrey, Sussex and Essex, and Mr Detmar Blow in the characteristic flint districts of Wiltshire.'

LETCHWORTH, HERTFORDSHIRE

Although garden suburbs were beginning to burgeon in the late 19th century, it was not until 1903 that the first garden city was planned at Letchworth by Barry Parker and Raymond Unwin, less than forty miles from London. A competitive exhibition of cheap prototype cottages for the rural labourer was held here and many architects took part. Tanglewood, in the not so cheap range, was designed by H.M.Baillie Scott in 1906 and was aimed at a new type of cottage owner, the 'weekender'. Baillie Scott was one of fourteen children of a rich Scotsman, and established an extremely successful Arts and Crafts domestic practice. He was influenced by Voysey in his simple and romantically sweeping roof lines, but his interiors were highly individual and sometimes highly exotic.

DORMANS LAND, LINGFIELD, SURREY

Although one-storey cottages were looked down on, the name 'bungalow' (a Hindu word meaning 'belonging to Bengal') made them perfectly all right again, and the Arts and Crafts architect Robert Briggs – 'a slick draftsman, but in the flesh too frightful' – greatly favoured the style. He earned the nickname 'Bungalow Briggs', and he designed this recherché dwelling, Pleasaunce Cottage, in 1890 along with others at Dormans Land, formerly called Bellagio. Bellagio gained a notorious reputation in the early part of this century as a collection of love nests, where mistresses were set up at a conveniently discreet distance from the Metropolis.

BRYANTS PUDDLE, MILBORNE, DORSET

Sir Ernest Debenham, with the considerable wealth from his London drapery store behind him, was a great pioneer in the field of agriculture (he was knighted in 1931 for 'Services to Agriculture'). His revolutionary experiment, the Bladen Farms, begun in 1919, involved, among other things, rural repopulation and the building of 30 or 40 dwellings for farm workers in single, double and triple cottages. Halsey Ricardo had already built Debenham House, Addison Road, in 1905, and was a leading figure in Arts and Crafts architecture. Together with McDonald Gill he created a village in the authentic local materials of cob and thatch, and McDonald's brother, Eric Gill, designed a large war memorial to complete the Arts and Crafts picture.

Arts Council of Great Britain, The, *English Cottages and Small Farmhouses* (1975)

Barley, M.W. *The English Farmhouse and Cottage* (Routledge & Kegan Paul, 1961)

Brocklebank, Joan *Affpuddle in the County of Dorset* (Commin, 1968)

Brown, R.J. *The English Country Cottage* (Robert Hale, 1979)

Brunskill, R.W. *Illustrated Handbook of Vernacular Architecture* (Faber & Faber, 1970)

Burton, Anthony and Pratt, Derek *Canal* (David & Charles, 1976)

Cave, Lyndon F. *The Smaller English House* (Robert Hale, 1981)

Clew, Kenneth R. *The Dorset & Somerset Canal* (David & Charles, 1971)

Clifton-Taylor, Alec *The Pattern of English Building* (Faber & Faber, 1972)

Cobbett, William *Rural Rides* (1830)

Colvin, H.M. *Biographical Dictionary of English Architects 1660–1840* (John Murray, 1954)

Crookston, Peter *Village England* (Hutchinson, 1980)

Darley, Gillian *Villages of Vision* (Architectural Press, 1975)

Defoe, Daniel *A Tour Through The Whole Island Of Great Britain* (1724)

Ditchfield, P.H. *The Charm of the English Village* (1908)

Felkin, William *History of the Machine-Wrought Hosiery and Lace Manufactures* (David & Charles, 1967)

Girouard, Mark *Life in the English Country House* (Yale University Press, 1978)

Hardwick, Michael and Mollie *Writers' Houses* (Phoenix, 1968)

Highways and Byways series (Macmillan)

Hudson, W.H. *A Shepherd's Life* (Methuen, 1910)

Jones, Sydney R. *The Village Homes of England* (The Studio, 1912)

Laing, David *Hints for Dwellings* (1801)

Loudon, J.C. *Encyclopaedia of Cottage Architecture* (1836)

Mee, Arthur *The King's England* series (Hodder & Stoughton)

Mercer, Eric *English Vernacular Houses* (HMSO, 1975)

Morris, George L. and Wood, Esther *The Country Cottage* (Bodley Head, 1906)

National Trust, The, *Villages* (Heritage, 1978)

Neve, Richard *The City and Country Purchaser* (1726)

Pakington, Humphrey *English Villages and Hamlets* (Batsford, 1934)

Pearse Chope, R. *Early Tours in Devon and Cornwall* (1918)

Pocock, W.F. *Architectural Designs for Rustic Cottages and Picturesque Dwellings* (1807)

Ponting, Kenneth G. *The Woollen Industry of South-West England* (Adams & Dart, 1971)

Price, Uvedale *Essay on the Picturesque* (1794)

Prizeman, John *Your House: The Outside View* (Hutchinson, 1975)

Richardson, C.J. *The Englishman's House* (Chatto & Windus, 1888)

Samuel, Raphael *Village Life and Labour* (Routledge & Kegan Paul, 1975)

Service, Alastair *Edwardian Architecture* (Thames & Hudson, 1977)

Shell County Guides, The, (Faber & Faber)

Thompson, E.P. *The Making of the English Working Class* (Victor Gollancz, 1963)

Thompson, Flora *Lark Rise to Candleford* (Penguin Modern Classics, 1973)

Weaver, Lawrence *The 'Country Life' Book of Cottages* (Country Life Books, 1913)

Weinstock, M.B. *Old Dorset* (David & Charles, 1967)

Wiltshire Archaeological Magazine (1860)

Wood, John *Series of Plans For Cottages Or Habitations Of The Labourer* (1781)

Woodforde, John *The Truth about Cottages* (Routledge & Kegan Paul, 1979)